Selected Works of Louis-Auguste Blanqui
2011 EatDogEat Publishing

Selected Works of Louis-Auguste Blanqui

Contents

Appeal to the Students

To the students of law and medicine,

Benjamin Constant has died. France weeps for one of the firmest upholders of its freedom, a great citizen and a great man. For us, it is a for friend that we weep. You know the accents his voice found to repulse the calumnies and insults poured upon us by an oppressive power. You know what burning words he made heard in 1820, 1821, 1822 and 1827, when, not content to sacrifice us to the sword of their hirelings, the powerful insulted us from the tribune and in their newspapers. Benjamin Constant made it a point of pride to be the friend of young people. Until his last moment, he raised his voice to defend us, because the youth of France, just as much as freedom, needed to be defended, even after the battle of the July Days. Five days before his death, the assembly halls still resounded to his patriotic tones; he died in battle as a combatant for the principles and the achievements of our revolution. An entire people will accompany the mortal remains of the defender of our rights to his last resting place. The Colleges owe to their friend a particular mourning, a solemn homage of recognition. I invite all my comrades to meet on the place du Pantheon, Sunday at precisely nine o'clock in the morning. Those of you who have weapons shall come armed, in order to render Benjamin Constant funeral honours.

Louis-Auguste Blanqui,

Student of Law

P.S. – General Lafayette has given approval to this meeting; one of his staff officers will go along with us tomorrow.

7

Reception Procedure of the Society of the Seasons

The newly-elected member is brought in blindfolded.

The president to the presenter: What is the name of the new brother you bring us...

To the newly-elected member: Citizen (...) What is your age? Your profession? Your birthplace? Your home? How do you earn a living?

Have you thought through the step you take at this time, the engagement to which you commit yourself? Do you know that traitors are struck down dead?

Swear, Citizen, to reveal to no one what happens in this place.

The president poses the following questions.

– 1 What do you think of royalty and of kings?

That they are as dangerous to humanity as the tiger is to other animals.

– 2 What are aristocrats now?

Aristocracy by birth was abolished in July 1830. It was replaced by the aristocracy of money, which is every bit as voracious as the preceding one.

– 3 Should we be satisfied with overthrowing royalty?

All aristocrats must be overthrown, all privileges must be abolished

– 4 What must we put in its place?

The government of the people by the people, which is to

9

say, the republic.

– 5 Those who have rights without fulfilling obligations, as is the case with aristocrats, are they part of the people?

They ought not to be part of the people; they are to the social what a cancer is to the human body: the first condition for the return of the social body to a just state is the wiping out of aristocracy.

– 6 Can the people immediately govern themselves immediately after the revolution?

The social state being gangrened, heroic remedies are required to pass to a healthy state; the people will need, for a certain period of time, a revolutionary power.

– 7 In summary, what are your principles?

Royalty and all aristocracies must be exterminated; to substitute in their place the republic, which is to say the government of equality; but, to pass to this government, to employ a revolutionary power, which sets the people to exercise its rights.

Citizen, the principles which you have just expressed are the only correct ones, the only ones that can make humanity march towards the goal which is fixed for it; but their realization isn't easy. Our enemies are numerous and powerful; they have at their disposition all of society's forces: we republicans have only our courage and our conviction. You still have time, think of all the dangers to which you expose yourself in entering our ranks: the sacrifice of fortune, the loss of freedom, perhaps death. Are you determined to brave these dangers?

Your response is the proof of your energy. Rise, Citizen, and take the following vow:

"In the name of the republic, I swear eternal hatred to all kings, all aristocrats, to all of humanity's oppressors. I swear absolute devotion to the people, fraternity to all men, aside from aristocrats; I swear to punish traitors; I promise to give my life, to go to the scaffold, if this sacrifice is necessary to bring about the reign of popular sovereignty and equality."

The president puts a dagger in his hand.

"Let me be punished with the death of traitors, let me be stabbed with this dagger if I violate this vow. I agree to be treated as a traitor if I reveal the least thing to anyone at all, even my closest relative, if he is not member of the association."

The president: Citizen, be seated; the Society receives your vow; you are now part of the association; work with others to free the people.

Citizen, your name will not be pronounced among us; here is your registration number in the workshop. You must procure arms, ammunition. The Committee which the society directs will remain unknown until the moment we take up arms. Citizen, one of your obligations is to spread the principles of the association. If you know any devoted and discreet citizens, you should present them to us.

The newly elected member is returned to the light.

Call to Arms

Art 1 – All citizens from 16 to 50 years of age are called upon for the defense of the fatherland and of freedom.

Art 2 – Men between 16-30 tears of age, armed or unarmed, are to report to the Place de l'Hotel de Ville in order to be organized in battalions.

Art 3 – Men between 30- 50 shall remain in their neighborhoods in order to prepare resistance there.

Art 4 – Barricades shall be constructed every 50 meters on all streets. The stones should be removed and on the principal streets the stones should be taken to the upper floors in order to be thrown at the troops of Charles X.

Art 5 – Former military men, officers, non-commissioned officers and soldiers are called to the Hotel de Ville in order to form the cadres of the popular battalions.

Art 6 – Commissions will be established for: 1 – provisioning, 2 – armament, 3 – supplying of ammunition. Citizens capable of fulfilling these functions are asked to present themselves to the Hotel de Ville.

Art 7 – Armorers shall deliver firearms, powder and bullets found in their stores to the people. The state will reimburse them for the price of these objects with a 25% bonus for the risks involved.

Speech before the Society of the Friends of the People

The fact shouldn't be hidden that there is a war to the death between the classes that compose the nation. This truth recognized, the truly national party, the ones patriots should rally to, is the party of the masses.

Until now there have been three interests in France: that of the so-called upper classes, that of the middle or bourgeois class, and finally that of the people. I place the people last because they were always the last and because I count on an imminent application of the Gospel maxim that "the last shall be first."

In 1814 and 1815 the bourgeois class, tired of Napoleon not because of despotism (it cares little for liberty, which in its eyes it isn't worth a pound of good cinnamon or a nice fat bill), but because the blood of the people being exhausted, the war was beginning to take its children from it and, even more, because it harmed its tranquility and hindered commerce. The bourgeois class then received the foreign soldiers as liberators and the Bourbons as God's envoys. They were the ones who opened the gates of Paris, who treated the soldiers of Waterloo as brigands, and who encouraged the bloody reaction of 1815.

Louis XVIII rewarded them with the Charter. This Charter established the upper classes as an aristocracy and gave the bourgeois the Chamber of Deputies, called the democratic chamber. With this the émigrés, the nobles, the big landowners who were fanatical partisans of the Bourbons, and the middle class who accepted them from self-interest found themselves the masters in equal part of the government. The people were pushed to the side. Bereft of leaders, demoralized by foreign invasion, having lost faith in liberty, they remained silent and submitted to the yoke while remaining on their guard. You know the consistent support the bourgeois class gave the Restoration until 1825. It loaned its hand to the massacres of 1815 and 1816, to the scaffolds of Borie and Berton, to the war in Spain, to the arrival of Villèle and the changes in the electoral law; until 1827 it regularly sent majorities given over to those in power.

In the period 1825-1827 Charles X, seeing that he was succeeding at everything and believing himself strong enough without the bourgeois, wanted to proceed to their exclusion, as was done with the people in 1815. He took a daring step towards the *Ancien Régime* and declared war on the middle class by proclaiming the exclusive dominance of the nobility and clergy under the banner of Jesuitism. The bourgeoisie is by essence anti-spiritual: it detests churches, and believes only in double entry bookkeeping. The priests irritated them: they had consented to share with the upper classes in oppressing the people, but seeing its turn arrive as well, full of resentment and jealousy against the high aristocracy, it rallied to that minority of the middle class that had combated the Bourbons since 1815 and that it had sacrificed up till then. It was then that a war of newspapers and elections began, carried out with so much steadfastness and fury. But the bourgeois fought in the name of the Charter and nothing but the Charter, and in fact the Charter assured their power. Faithfully executed, it gave them supremacy within the state. Legality was invented to represent this interest of the bourgeoisie's and to serve as its flag. The legal order became a kind of divinity before which constitutional opponents burned their daily incense. This struggle was carried out from 1825 -1830, ever more favorably to the bourgeois, who rapidly gained ground and who, masters of the Chamber of Deputies, soon threatened the government with complete defeat.

What were the people doing in the midst of this conflict? Nothing. They remained a silent spectator to the quarrel, and everyone knows that its interests didn't count in the debates of its oppressors. To be sure, the bourgeois cared little about them and their cause, which were looked on as having been lost fifteen years before. You recall that the papers most devoted to the constitutionals regularly repeated that the people had submitted their resignation to their representatives, the only organs of France. It wasn't only the government that considered the masses as indifferent to the debate: the middle classes detested them perhaps even more, and they surely counted on being the only ones to pluck the fruits of victory. That victory didn't go further than the Charter. Charles X and the Charter with an all-powerful bourgeoisie, this was the goal of the constitutionals. Yes, but the people understood the question differently. The people mocked the Charter in execrating the Bourbons. Seeing its masters argue among themselves it spied out in silence the moment to leap onto the battlefield and bring the parties into agreement.

When the classes arrived at such a point that the government no longer had any resource than coups d'état, and that that threat of a coup d'état was suspended over the heads of the bourgeois, then they were gripped with fear! Who doesn't recall the regrets and terrors of the 221 after the order of dissolution that answered their famous address? Charles X spoke of his firm resolve to resort to force, and the bourgeoisie blanched. Already most of them loudly disapproved the 221 for having allowed themselves to be carried away by revolutionary excesses. The most daring placed their hope in the refusal of a tax that would have been paid and in the support of tribunals, almost all of who would gladly have filled the office of summary political courts. If the royalists demonstrated so much confidence and resolution, if their adversaries showed so much fear and uncertainty, it's that both regarded the people as having resigned themselves and expected to find them neutral in the battle. And so on one hand the government depended on the nobility, the clergy and the big landowners, and on the other was the middle class which, after five years of warming up in a war of words, was ready to come to blows with the people, silent for fifteen years and believed resigned.

It was in these conditions that the combat was engaged.

The ordinances were issued and the police smashed the newspaper presses. I won't speak of our joy, citizens, we who are shaking the yoke and who are finally witnessing the reawakening of the popular lion that had slept for so long. July 26 was the most beautiful day of our life. But the bourgeois! Never has a political crisis offered a spectacle of such frightful, such profound consternation. Pale, frantic they heard the first shots as the first discharge of a picket that was to shoot them down one by one. You all remember the conduct of the deputies on Monday, Tuesday and Wednesday. They used what presence of mind and faculties fear left to them to ward off, to halt the combat. Preoccupied with their own cowardice, they were unready to foresee popular victory and were already trembling beneath Charles X's knife. But on Thursday the scene changed. The people were the victors. And then another terror seized them, more profound and oppressive. Farewell dreams of the Charter, of legality, of constitutional royalty, of the exclusive domination of the bourgeoisie! The powerless ghost that was Charles X faded away. In the midst of the debris, of flames and smoke, the people appeared standing on the corpse of royalty, standing like a giant, the tricolor flag in hand. They were struck with stupor. It was then that they regretted that the National Guard didn't exist July 26, that they condemned the lack of foresight and the folly of Charles X, who had smashed the anchor of his own salvation. It is too late for regrets! You can see that during these days, when the people were so grand, the bourgeois were tied up between two fears, that of Charles X in the first place, and then that of the workers. A noble and glorious role for these proud warriors who float their high plumes at parades on the Champ de Mars.

But citizens: how is it that so sudden and fearsome a revelation of the force of the masses remained sterile? By what fatality did that revolution made by the people alone, and that should have marked the end of the exclusive reign of the bourgeoisie as well as the success of popular interests and might, have no other results than the establishing of the despotism of the middle class, aggravating the poverty of the workers and peasants, and plunging France a bit further into the mud? Alas, the people, like the other old man, knew how to win, but not how to profit from its victory. The fault is not all their own. The combat was so brief that its natural leaders, those who would have led the way to victory, didn't have the time to distinguish themselves from the crowd. They necessarily rallied to the leaders who had figured at the head of the bourgeoisie in the parliamentary struggle against the Bourbons. What is more, they were grateful to the middle classes for their little five year war against their enemies, and you have seen what benevolence, I would almost say what feeling of deference they showed towards those men in suits they met on the streets after the battle. That cry of "Long Live the Charter!" which was so perfidiously abused was nothing but a rallying cry for proving its alliance with these men. Did they already feel, as if by instinct, that they had just played a nasty trick on the bourgeoisie and, in the generosity of the victor, did they want to make advances and offer peace and friendship to their future adversaries? Whatever the case, the masses hadn't formally expressed any positive political will. What acted on them, what had thrown them into the public square, was the hatred of the Bourbons, the firm resolution to overthrow them. There was both Bonapartism and the Republic in the wishes they formed for the government that was to issue from the barricades.

You know how the people, in its confidence in the chiefs they'd accepted and which their ancient hostility to Charles X made them consider them as equally implacable enemies of the entire Bourbon family, retired from the public squares once the battle was finished. At that point the bourgeois came out of their cellars and threw themselves in their thousands onto the streets, which the departure of the combatants had left free. There is no one who doesn't remember with what amazing suddenness the scene changed on the streets of Paris, like at a theatre; the way suits replaced work jackets, in the blink of an eye, as if a fairy wand had made some disappear and others spring up. This was because the bullets were no longer flying. It was no longer a question of receiving blows, but of gathering up loot. To each his role: the men of the workshops disappeared, the men who work behind the counter appeared.

It was then that the wretches who had been given victory as a deposit, after having attempted to place Charles X back on his throne, feeling that their lives were at risk and lacking the courage to brave the dangers of such a treason, stopped at a less perilous treason. A Bourbon was proclaimed king. Under the direction of agents paid with royal gold 10-15,000 bourgeois put in place in the courts of the new palace saluted the master for a few days with their cries of enthusiasm. As for the people, since they have no dividends and lack the means to stroll beneath the windows of palaces, they were in the workshops. But they weren't accomplices in this unworthy usurpation that would not have occurred had they found men capable of guiding their angry and vengeful blows. Betrayed by their chiefs, abandoned by the schools, they remained silent and on their guard, as in 1815. I'll cite you as an example a coachman who drove me last Saturday. After having told me of the part he played in the combats of the three days he added: " On the way to the Chamber I encountered the procession of deputies headed towards the Hotel de Ville. I followed them to see what they'd do. Then I saw Lafayette appear on the balcony with Louis-Philippe and say, 'Frenchmen, here is your King.' Sir, when I heard that word it was as if I'd been stabbed. I was blinded; I went on my way." That man is the people.

This then was the situation of the parties immediately following the July Revolution. The upper class was crushed; the middle class, which hid itself during the combat and disapproved it, demonstrating as much cleverness as it did prudence, snatched the fruits of victory that were won despite them. The people, who did everything, remained a zero, as before. But a terrible act has been accomplished: like a thunderbolt, the people had suddenly entered the political scene that they took by assault, and though more or less chased from it at the same instant, they nevertheless acted with mastery. They withdrew their resignation. It will henceforth be between them and the middle class that bitter war will be carried out. It's no longer between the upper classes and the bourgeois: in order to better resist, the latter will need to call their former enemies to their assistance. In fact, for a long time the bourgeoisie has not hidden its hatred of the people.

If we examine the conduct of the government there is in its policies, the same march, the same progression of hatred and violence as among the bourgeoisie, whose interests and passions it represents.

When the bricks of the barricades were still piled up in the streets all that was spoken of was the program of the Hotel de Ville, of republican institutions; handshakes, popular proclamations, the grand words of liberty, independence, and national glory were bandied about. And then, when those in power had at their disposal an organized military force, pretensions mounted; all the laws, all the ordinances of the Restoration were invoked and applied. Later, the prosecution of the press, the persecutions of the men of July, the people beaten and tracked down with bayonet blows, taxes increased and collected with a rigor unheard of under the Restoration: this entire apparatus of tyranny revealed the governments hatreds and fears. But it felt that the people felt that same hatred for them, and not judging itself strong enough with the support of the bourgeoisie alone it sought to rally the upper classes to its cause in order that, established on this dual base, it would be in a state to more successfully resist the threatened invasion of the proletarians. It is to this maneuver to conciliate the aristocracy that we should attach the system it has developed in the past eighteen months. This is the key to its policy. And this upper class is almost entirely composed of royalists. In order to bring them along it was thus necessary to as nearly as possible approach the Restoration, to follow its meanderings, to continue them. And this is what was done. Nothing was changed except the name of the king. The people's sovereignty was denied, trod upon. The court wore mourning attire for foreign princes, legitimacy was copied in all regards. Royalists were maintained in their places, and all those who had to leave in the first onrush of the revolution found more lucrative positions; the magistracy was preserved in such a way that the whole administration is in the hands of men devoted to the Bourbons. What is more, a part of this upper class, the most rotten part of it, that which above all wants gold and pleasures, deigned to promise its protection to public order. But the other part, the one I'll call the least rotted in order not to say " honorable," that which has self-respect and faith in its opinions, which worships its flag and its old memories, these people reject with disgust the caresses of the middle way. They have behind them the largest part of the populations of the south and the west, all those peasants of the Vendée and Brittany who, having remained foreign to the movement of civilization, preserve an ardent faith in Catholicism, and with reason confound in their devotions Catholicism with legitimacy, for these are two things that have lived and must die together.

Do you think that these simple and believing men are open to the seductions of bankers? No, citizens! For the people, whether if in their ignorance they are enflamed with religious fanaticism or if, more enlightened, they allow themselves to be carried away by enthusiasm for liberty, the people are ever great and generous; they don't obey low monetary interests but the nobler passions of the soul, the aspirations of elevated morality. But however delicately and deferentially we might handle Brittany and the Vendée, they are still ready to rise at the cry of "God and King" and threaten the government with their Catholic and royal armies, which the first shock will smash. And that's not all: that faction of the upper classes that attached itself to the middle way will abandon it at the first moment. All they promised was to not work to overthrow them. As for devotion, you know it's possible to have it towards coupon clippers. Even more, I'd say that the greatest part of the bourgeois, who are pressing, gathering around the government from hatred of the people who they fear, from fright at war, which they have a horror of for they think it'll take their *écus* from them, these bourgeois barely care for the current order; they feel it to be powerless to protect them. Let the white flag [of the Royalists] come along that would guarantee them the oppression of the people and material security and they'd be ready to sacrifice their former political pretensions, for they bitterly regret having, through pride, sapped the power of the Bourbons and prepared their fall. They would abdicate their part of power to the hands of the aristocracy, willingly trading tranquility for servitude.

For the government of Louis-Philippe hardly reassures them. It can copy the Restoration all it wants, persecute patriots, set itself to erasing the stain of insurrection it is soiled with in the eyes of the adorers of public order. The memory of those three terrible days pursues them, dominates them. Eighteen months of successful war against the people were unable to counter-balance one sole popular victory. The battlefield is still theirs and that already old victory is suspended over power's head like the sword of Damocles. All are looking to see if the thread is not soon going to break.

Citizens, two principles share France, that of legitimacy and that of popular sovereignty. The first is the ancient organization of the past. This is the framework society lived in for 1400 years, and that some want to preserve by instinct of self-preservation, and others because they fear that the framework won't be able to be promptly replaced and anarchy will follow its dissolution. The principle of popular sovereignty rallies all men of the future, the masses who, tired of being exploited, seek to smash the framework that suffocates them. There is no third flag, no middle term. The middle road is foolishness, a bastard government that wants to give itself airs of legitimacy that one can only laugh at. And so the royalists, who perfectly understand

23

this situation, profit from the tact and indulgence of those in power who seek to bring them over to them so as to more actively work at their destruction. Their many newspapers demonstrate daily that the only possible order is legitimacy, that the middle road is powerless to constitute the country, that apart from legitimacy there is only revolution and once the first has been left behind, there is only the second.

What will then happen? The upper classes are waiting for the moment to raise the white flag. In the middle class the great majority, composed of those men who have no other homeland than their counter or their cash box, who would gladly become Russian, Prussian, or English to earn two *liards* on a piece of cloth or 1/4 % additional profit on discount, will without fail line themselves up behind the white flag. The very name of war and popular sovereignty makes them tremble. The minority of that class, made up of intellectual professions and the small number of bourgeois who love the tricolor flag, the symbol of France's independence and freedom, will take the side of popular sovereignty.

What is more, the moment of disaster is rapidly approaching. You see that the Chamber of Peers, the magistracy, and most civil servants are openly conspiring for the return of Henri V, mocking the middle road. Legitimist gazettes no longer hide either the hopes or the projects of the counter-revolution. The royalists in Paris and the provinces are gathering their forces, organizing the Vendée and Brittany, and are proudly planting their banner. They are openly saying that the bourgeoisie is with them, and they aren't wrong. They are only waiting for a signal from foreign lands to raise the white banner, for in foreign countries they would be crushed by the people. They know this and we are counting on their being crushed, even with foreign support.

You can be assured Citizens that they will not want for this support. This is the place to take a look at our relations with the European powers. It should be noted, in fact, that the external situation has developed in parallel with the political march of the government internally. External shame has grown in the exact same proportion as bourgeois despotism and the poverty of the masses internally.

At the first sound of our revolution the kings lost their heads, and the electric spark of insurrection having rapidly set Belgium, Poland, and Italy aflame, they sincerely thought their last day had arrived. How could it be imagined that the revolution didn't mean a revolution, that the expulsion of the Bourbons didn't mean the expulsion of the Bourbons, that the overturning of the Restoration would be a new edition of the Restoration? Not even the maddest of individuals could believe this. The cabinets saw in the three days the awakening of the French people and the beginning of its vengeance against the oppressors of nations. Nations judged in the same way as cabinets. But for our friends and enemies it was soon obvious that France had fallen into the hands of cowardly merchants who asked only to traffic in its independence and to sell its glory and liberty at the best price possible. While the kings awaited our declaration of war they received begging letters in which the French government implored pardon for its errors. The new master excused himself for having participated against his will in the revolt. He protested his innocence and his hatred for the revolution that he promised to tame, to punish, to wipe out if his good friends the kings promised him their protection, a small place in the Holy Alliance whose faithful servant he would become.

The foreign cabinets understood that the people weren't complicit in this treason and that it wouldn't delay in rendering justice. Their decision was taken: exterminate the insurrections that had broken out in Europe, and when everything returns to order unite their forces against France and come strangle in Paris itself the revolution and the revolutionary agent. This plan was followed with an admirable consistency and skill. They couldn't go too fast, because the people of July, still full of their recent triumph, would have been too alert to a too direct threat and would have forced its government's hand. In any event, it was necessary to grant time to the middle way to stifle enthusiasm, discourage patriots and instill mistrust and discord in the nation. They also couldn't go too slowly, for the masses could have grown tired of the servitude and poverty that weighed on it internally and for a second time smash the yoke before the foreigners were in shape.

All of these shoals were avoided. The Austrians invaded Italy. The bourgeois who govern us said "Good!" and bowed before Austria. The Russians exterminated Poland. Our government cried "Very good!" and prostrated itself before Russia. During this time the London conference amused the onlookers with its protocols aimed at assuring the independence of Belgium, for a Restoration in Belgium would have opened France's eyes and it would have been in a position to defend its work. The kings are now taking a forward step. They don't want an independent Belgium: it's a Dutch restoration they want to impose on it. The three courts of the north, confronted with the massacre, refuse to ratify the famous treaty that cost the conference sixteen months of labor.

And now will the middle way respond with a declaration of war on this insolent aggression. War! Good God! The word makes the bourgeois turn pale. Listen to them! War means bankruptcy, war means the Republic! War can only be supported with the blood of the people; the bourgeoisie doesn't involve itself in this. Their interests, their passions have to be appealed to in the name of liberty, of the fatherland's independence. The country must be put back into their hands, which alone can save it. It would be a hundred times better to see the Russians in Paris than to unleash the passions of the multitude. At least the Russians are friends of order; they reestablished order in Warsaw... These are calculations and the language of the middle way.

The Royalists will keep themselves at the ready, and next spring the Russians, on crossing the border, will find their lodgings prepared for them as far as Paris. For you can be sure that when the time comes the bourgeoisie will not resolve to make war. Its terror will have been increased by all the fear that will be inspired in it by the anger of a people betrayed and sold out, and you'll see the merchants brandish the white rosette and receive the enemy as a liberator, for the Cossacks frighten them less than the mob in work jackets.

Defence Speech of the Citizen Louis-Auguste Blanquibefore the Court Of Assizes

Messrs Jurors,

I am accused of having said to thirty million French people, proletarians like me, that they had the right to live. If that is a crime, then it seems to me at least that I should answer for it not to judges and prosecutors. However, Messrs, note well that the Prosecuting Attorney did not address himself to your sense of equity and your reason, but to your passions and your interests; he did not call on you to be strict in responding to a breach of morals and the laws; he only seeks to unleash vengeance against what he represents to you as a threat to your existence and your property. I am thus not in front of judges, but in the presence of enemies; so it would be quite useless to defend myself. Also, I have no fear of any sentence that you may pass on me, while protesting nevertheless with energy against this substitution of violence for justice, for this frees me in the future of any inhibition against repaying the law with force. However, if it is my duty as a proletarian, deprived of all the rights of the city, to reject the competence of a court where only the privileged classes who are not my peers sit in judgment over me, I am convinced that you have enough courage to appreciate with dignity the role which honor imposes on you in a circumstance where more or less disarmed adversaries are delivered to you for execution. As for our role, it is written in advance; the role of accuser is the only one which is appropriate for the oppressed.

For one should not imagine that men who have today fraudulently been given a one-day power by stealth and fraud, can drag, at their will, patriots before their justice, and by showing us the blade, force us to beg mercy for our patriotism.

Do not believe that we came here to justify the offences for which we are charged! Far from it! We are honored by this charge, and it is an honor to sit today on the same bench with criminals, for we will launch our charges against the wretched ones who have ruined and dishonored France, while waiting for the natural order of the opposing benches be restored in this court, and in which accusers and accused are in their true place.

What I will say will explain why we wrote the lines for which we are accused by the Crown, and why we will continue write more still.

The Prosecuting Attorney has, so to speak, summoned before your imaginations the a revolt of the slaves, in order, by fear, to excite your hatred: "You see," he says, "it is the war of the poor against the rich; all those who have property must repel the invasion. We bring you your enemies; strike them now, before they become any more fearsome!"

Yes, Messrs, this is the war between the rich and the poor: the rich wanted it thus, because they are the aggressors. Only they find it evil that the poor fight back; they would readily say in speaking of the people "This animal is so ferocious that it defends itself when attacked." The entire philippic of Mr. Prosecuting Attorney is summed up in this one sentence.

They never cease denouncing the proletarians as robbers ready to throw themselves on the men of property: why? Because they complain of being crushed by taxes for the profit of the privileged classes. *As for the privileged, who live in luxury on the sweat of the proletariat*, they are legal owners of property who are threatened with plunder by a greedy populace. It is not the first time that executioners take on the air of victims. Who are then, these robbers worthy of so much of hatred and torment? Thirty million French people who pay to the tax department a billion and half, and about an equal amount to the privileged classes. And the people of property who live off the labors of the whole society, they are two or three hundred thousand idlers who peacefully devour the billion paid by these "robbers." It seems to me that it is here, in a new form, and between other adversaries, that we find the war of the feudal barons against the merchants they robbed on the highways.

In fact, the present government does not have any other base apart from this iniquitous distribution of benefits and burdens. The restoration of 1814 was instituted courtesy of foreigners, with the aim of enriching an imperceptible minority by depriving the rest of the nation. One hundred thousand bourgeois form what is called, by a bitter irony, the "democratic element." What, good God, are the other elements *Paul Courier already immortalized the "representative machine"; this suction-and-force pump which compresses the mass called the people, to suck out of them milliards which flow continuously into the coffers of idlers, this pitiless machine which crushes one by one, twenty-five million peasants and five million workers to draw out the purest extract of their blood and to transfuse it into the veins of the privileged.* The wheels of this machine, combined with a marvelous art, reach the poor at every moment of the day, intruding into every moment of their humble life, taking a cut of their smallest earnings, the most miserable of their pleasures. And it is not enough that such an amount of money travels from the pockets of the proletarians to those to the wealthy in passing through the abysses of the tax department; more enormous sums still are raised directly from the masses by the privileged classes, by means of the laws which govern industrial and commercial transactions, laws which these same privileged people have the exclusive right to make for themselves.

In order for the large-scale landowner to draw from his fields a high rent, foreign corn is hit by an import duty which increases the price of the bread; well, you know a few centimes more or less on a loaf of bread is life or death for thousands of workers. The grain law hits especially hard the maritime population of the south. To enrich some large manufacturers and the owners of forests, iron from Germany and Sweden is subject to enormous duty, so that the peasants are forced to buy bad tools at high cost, while they could get the excellent ones at a cheap rate; the foreigner in his turn avenges himself for our prohibitions by pushing French wine out of his markets, which, together with the taxes which weigh on this food product inside the country, reduces the richest regions of France to misery, and strangling the wine industry, the most natural industry of this country, a truly indigenous form of cultivation, which promotes the enrichment of the soil and favors small-scale property. I will not speak about the tax on salt, the lottery, the tobacco monopoly, in a word, this inextricable network of taxes, monopolies, prohibitions, customs duties and government contracts. Who enchains and atrophies its members? Suffice to say that this mass of taxes is always to distributed so as to benefit the rich, and to weigh exclusively on the poor, or rather that *the idlers practice a shameful plundering of the masses*. Plundering is essential indeed.

Doesn't one need a large civil list to pay the cost of the royal family, to console it for the sublime sacrifice which it has made of its peace and quiet for the happiness of the country? And, since one of the principal titles of the junior Bourbons to heredity consists in its numerous family, the State will not act in a petty fashion and will not refuse privileges for the princes and dowries for the princesses. There is also this immense army of sinecurists, of diplomats, and civil servants for whom France, for its happiness, must provide a huge budget, so that they can enrich by their luxury the privileged bourgeoisie, because all the money of these contributing to the budget is spent in the cities, and should not turn over to the peasants even one penny of the billion and half of which they pay the five-sixths.

Isn't it necessary also that this new financial star, this Gil Blas of the 19th century, courtier and apologist of all the ministries, favourite of the Count d'Olivarès as of the Duke of Lerme, sell high offices for great lumps of cash? It is essential to lubricate the large wheels of the representative machine, to richly endow brothers, nephews, cousins. And shouldn't the courtiers, the courtesans, the intriguers, the croupiers who gamble the honor and future of the country on the Stock Exchange, the middle-men, the mistresses, the dealers, the informers, those who speculate on the fall of Poland, all this vermin of the palaces and the salons, mustn't they all be gorged on gold? Shouldn't one promote the fermentation of this manure that so successfully fertilizes public opinion?

Here we have a government that the silver tongues of the ministry present to us as the masterpiece of all systems of social organisation, the summation of all that was good and perfect in the various administrative mechanisms since the flood; here are what they praise as the last word in human perfectibility as regards government! It is all nothing more than the theory of corruption pushed to its outer limits. The strongest proof that this order of things is instituted only for the exploitation of the poor by the rich, that they have sought no other base than an ignoble and brutal materialism, is the parochial idiocy which grips their minds. Indeed, this is a guarantee of morality, and the morality inadvertently introduced into such a system could enter there only as an infallible element of destruction.

I ask, Messrs, how men of noble heart and intelligence, rejected as pariahs by the aristocracy of wealth, would not resent such a cruel insult? How could they remain indifferent to the shame of their country, to the suffering of the proletariat, their brothers in misfortune? Their duty is to invite the masses to smash the yoke of misery and ignominy; this duty I have fulfilled in spite of imprisonment; we will fulfil this duty until the end by facing our enemies. When one has behind oneself a great people that is marching to the conquest of its welfare and its freedom, one must know how to throw oneself into the trenches as an inspiration and to make for it a way forward.

The ministerial organs repeat with kindness that there are ways open to the complaints of the proletarians, that the laws present regular means for to them to pursue their interests. This is an insult. The tax department is there, which hounds them its insatiable appetite; it must work, work night and day incessantly in order to ceaselessly throw feed to the ever-reborn hunger of this chasm; quite happy if there remains to them some scraps to disguise the hunger of their children. The people do not write in the newspapers; they do not send petitions to the chambers: it would be a waste of time. Much more, all the voices which have repercussion in the political sphere, the voices of the salons, those of the boutiques, of the cafés, in a word of all the places where what is called the public opinion is formed, these voices are those of the privileged; not one of these voices belongs to the people; it is mute; it vegetates far from these high areas where its destiny is determined. When, by chance, the tribune or the press lets escape some words of pity about the misery of the people, they hasten to impose silence in the name of public safety, which forbids touching upon these extreme questions, or such talk is declared to be anarchy. If someone persists, prison renders justice to this rabble-rousing which disturbs the ministerial digestion. And then, when there is a great silence, they say: "See, France is happy, it is peaceful: order reigns! ..."

But in spite of all these precautions the cry of hunger, emitted by thousands of poor wretches, reaches the ears of the privileged classes, they howl, they exclaim: "Force must remain with the law! The only passion a nation should feel is for the law!" So Messrs, according to you, all laws are good? Have you never come across a law that struck horror into you? Do you not know of any law that is ridiculous, odious or immoral? Is it possible to be so cut off behind an abstract word, a word that refers to a chaos of forty thousand laws, among which there is both the best and the worst? You answer: "If there are bad laws, ask for legal reform; but in the meantime obey..." This is an even more bitter insult. The laws are made by a hundred thousand voters, applied by a hundred thousand magistrates, carried out by a hundred thousand urban national guards, because you have deliberately disorganized the national guard in the countryside because they are too close to the people. However these voters, these jurors, these national guards, they are the same individuals, who accumulate the most opposed functions and are all at the same time legislators, judges and soldiers, so that the same man in the morning created a deputy, that is, the law, applies law at midday in his capacity as a juror, and carries it out in the evening in the street in the costume of the national guard. What do the thirty million proletarians do in all these transformations? They pay.

The apologists of the representative government have mainly founded their praises for this system on the separation of the three powers: legislative, legal and executive. They cannot think of enough words of praise for this marvelous balance that has solved the longstanding problem of reconciling order with freedom, of movement with stability. *Eh bien!* That is precisely what the representative system is, exactly as the apologists describe it, which concentrates the three powers in the hands of a small number of privileged people all linked by the same interests. Is this not a confusion that constitutes the most monstrous of tyrannies, by the very avowal of its apologists, so that there isn't any confusion about what constitutes the most monstrous of tyrannies, by the admission of these same apologists?

So what is the upshot? The proletarian remains on the outside. The Deputies, elected by the monopolists of power, imperturbably continue their manufacture of tax laws, penal codes, administrative regulations, all directed with a same aim of exploitation. Now that are the people going about, shouting of their hunger, demanding of the elite that they abdicate their privileges, of the monopolists that they give up their monopoly, and of all of them to renounce their idleness, they will laugh at them, looking down their noses at them. What would the nobility have done in 1789 if one had humbly begged them to give up their feudal rights? They would have punished the people's insolence... Things are done differently now.

The most skilful of this gutless aristocracy, sensing all that is threatening to them in the despair of a starving multitude, propose to reduce the misery of the people a little, not for reasons of humanity, God forbid! But to reduce the danger. As for political rights, one cannot say anything of them, it is only a question of throwing the proletarians a bone to gnaw upon.

Other men, with better intentions, pretend that the people are tired of freedom and only ask to live. I do not know what whim of despotism impels them to exalt the example of Napoleon, who knew how to rally the masses by giving them bread in exchange for freedom. It is true that this populist dictator was supported for a time, particularly because he tried to flatter the passion of egalitarianism, and because he shot corrupt traders, who would today be penalized by being made deputies. He didn't perish any the less for having killed freedom. This is a valuable lesson for those who want to follow in this tradition.

Today one cannot respond to the cries of distress from a starving population, by repeating the insulting words of Imperial Rome: *panem et circenses!* Let it be known that the people do not beg any more! There is no question of dropping from a splendid table some crumbs to amuse them; the people do not need alms; it intends to secure its well being by its own efforts. The people want to make and will make the laws that must govern them: then laws will no longer be made against them; they will be made for them because they will be made by them. We do not recognise the right of anyone to grant such generosities which a contrary whim could revoke. We ask that the thirty-three million French people choose the shape of their government, and name, by universal suffrage, the representatives who will have the mission of making laws. This reform accomplished, the taxes which strip the poor for the profit of the rich will be promptly destroyed and replaced by others established on a contrary base. Instead of taking from the hardest workers to give to the rich, taxes must seize the superfluity of the idlers to distribute it among the poor masses, condemned to unemployment because of the lack of money; taxes must hit the unproductive consumers so as to fertilize the sources of production; facilitate the reduction of the public debt, which is the ruin of the country; finally to substitute for the disastrous swindle of the Stock Exchange, a system of national banks where the active men will be able to find the capital they need. Then, but only then, will the taxes be a benefit.

Voilà, Messrs, that's what we mean by the republic, not otherwise. '93 is a bogeyman good for porters and domino players. Take note, Messrs, that it is quite intentionally that I pronounced these words 'universal suffrage', to show our contempt for certain *rapprochements*. We all know well that a government backed into a corner puts to work lies, calumnies, and ridiculous or perfidious tales to restore some credence to the old tale that it has been exploiting for such a long time, of an alliance between the republicans and the Carlists, that is, between things which are totally antithetical to each other. This is its only port in a storm, its great resource in finding some support. It can only find support by basing itself on such filth; and the most stupid conspiracy stories, the most odious farces invented by the police do not appear too dangerous a game for them if it manages to frighten France with Carlism, to turn it for a few days more from republicanism, where its instinct for salvation leads it. But what can persuade people of the possibility of this union against nature? Don't the Carlists have on their hands the blood of our friends who died on the scaffolds of the Restoration? We are not so forgetful of our martyrs. Isn't it against the revolutionary spirit, represented by the tricolor behind which the Bourbons assembled all Europe for twenty-five years, and behind which they still seek to assemble? This flag is not yours, apostles of quasi-legitimacy! it is that of the Republic! It is we, the republicans, who raised it in 1830, without you and in spite of you, who burned it in 1815; and Europe knows well that republican France only will defend it, when it is again attacked by the monarchy. If there is a natural alliance, it is between you and these Carlists; it's not that you are in agreement on the same man at the moment; they are holding on for theirs, who is not here yet; but you will sell yours cheaply, to be more accommodating, and to better arrive at that which you have in common with them, all the more because in doing so you do nothing but return to your old racket.

Indeed, the very word "Carlists" is nonsensical; they are, and can only be in France royalists and republicans. Political opinion divides itself every more sharply between these two principles; the good people who had believed in a third principle, some species of neutral kind called a "happy medium," are gradually giving up this absurdity, and will wriggle their way to one or the other flag, according to their passion and their interest. However, you, monarchists, who exude monarchy as you speak, everyone knows under which banner your doctrines belong. You did not wait eighteen months to choose it. On July 28, 1830, at ten o'clock in the morning, in the newspaper office, having said that I was going to get my rifle and my tricolor rosette, one of the today's powerful individuals exclaimed, filled with indignation: "Sir, the tricolor can well be yours, but they will be never mine; the white flag [of the royalty] is the flag of France." Then as now, these gentlemen held France with a small group.

Eh bien! We conspired fifteen years against the white flag, and it is with grinding teeth that we see it floating above the Tuileries and the Hôtel de Ville, where the foreigner had planted it. The most beautiful day of our life was when we dragged it through the mud of the gutters, and where we trampled underfoot the white rosette, this prostitute of the enemy camp. One needs a rare amount of impudence to throw in our face this charge of complicity with the royalists; and on another hand it is a clumsy hypocrisy to take pity on our alleged credulity, on our simplistic good-naturedness, which lead us, according to one of you, to be so easily deceived by the Carlists. If I speak thus, it is not to insult our enemies while they are down; they say that are strong, they have their Vendée; let them start up again, and we'll see what we'll see!

As to the rest, I repeat, one will soon have to choose

between the monarchical monarchy and the republican republic; we will see whom the majority support. Still, if the opposition in the Chamber of Deputies, as national as it is, cannot rally the whole country; if it allows the government to accuse it of incapacity and impotence, it's that even while clearly rejecting royalty, it hasn't dared declare itself, with the same frankness, for the republic; in saying what they did not want, they nevertheless did not articulate what they did want. It solves nothing to avoid using this word republic, with which the men of Corruption endeavor to frighten the nation, knowing well that the nation wants the republic almost unanimously. They have distorted history, for forty years, with incredible success, so as to frighten people; but the last eighteen months have corrected many errors, dissipated many lies, and the people will not much longer accept the situation. They want freedom and well-being. It is a calumny to represent it as a trade off, that the people must give up all their freedoms for a piece of bread: we must cast this imputation back at the political atheists who threw it. Is it not the people who, in all the crises, were ready to sacrifice their welfare and their lives for moral interests? Is it not the people who asked to die in 1814, rather than to see the foreigner in Paris? And yet what material need pushed it to this act of devotion? It had bread on April 1 as well as on March 30.

These privileged people, on the contrary, that one would have supposed so easy to stir up by the great ideas of Fatherland and Honor, due to the exquisite sensitivity that they owe to opulence; who could at least have calculated better than others the disastrous consequences of the foreign invasion; isn't it they who raised the white rosette in the presence of the enemy, and kissed the boots of the Cossack? What! Classes which applauded the dishonor of the country, which make a profession of the most disgusting materialism, which would sacrifice a thousand years of freedom, of prosperity and glory for a three day cease-fire purchased by infamy, these classes would have in their hands exclusive custody of national dignity ! Because corruption has made them made stupid, they recognize in the people only the appetites of beasts, in order to assume the right to allow them only such food as is necessary to maintain the people as fodder for them to exploit!

It is not hunger either which, in July, pushed the workers into the streets; they were motivated by sentiments of the loftiest morality, the desire to redeem themselves from servitude by rendering a great service to the country, and especially by the hatred of the Bourbons! Because the people never recognised the Bourbons; their hatred smoldered for fifteen years, waiting in silence for the chance of vengeance; and, when their strong hand smashed their yoke, they believed that they had torn up the treaties of 1815 at the same time. The thing is that the proletariat has a more profound political sense than the statesmen; its instinct told it that a nation does not have a future, so long its past is burdened with a shame of which it has not been cleansed. And so war! This does not mean that France should again embark on absurd conquests, but rather to raise France from its status as an outlaw, to restore its honor, the first condition of prosperity; War! in order to prove to our sister nations of Europe that, far from bearing a grudge for what was a fatal error both for us and for them, which led them to carry their arms into France in 1814, we could avenge both them and us by punishing the lying kings, and at the same time bring peace and freedom to our neighbors! This is what 30 million French people wanted when they greeted the new era with enthusiasm.

This should have been the outcome of the revolution of July. It came to serve as the complement to our forty revolutionary years. Under the Republic, the people had conquered freedom at the price of famine; the Empire gave them a kind of prosperity while stripping them of their freedom. The two regimes gloriously knew how to enhance dignity beyond our borders, the primary need for a great nation. All this perished in 1815, and this victory of the foreigners lasted fifteen years. So what was the battle of July, if not a revenge for this long defeat, and it revived again the bonds of our national feeling? And any revolution having been a step forward, shouldn't this one have assured us the complete enjoyment of those goods which we had till then only had partial enjoyment of, finally restoring to us all that which we had lost by the Restoration?

Freedom! Well-Being! National dignity! Such was the currency entered on the plebeian flag of 1830. The ultra-royalists read instead: *Maintenance of all the privileges! Charter of 1814! Quasi legitimacy!* In consequence, they gave to the people servitude and misery within our borders, and infamy beyond them. Did the proletariat thus fight just for a change of the effigy placed on these banknotes which they so seldom see? Are we at this point concerned with new medals, for which we have overturned thrones to bring such fantasies to pass? It is the opinion of a ministerial propagandist who swears that in July we *persisted in* demanding a constitutional monarchy, with the variant of Louis-Philippe in place of Charles X. The people, according to him, took part in the fight only as an instrument of the bourgeoisie; that is, that the proletarians are gladiators who kill and have themselves killed for the amusement and profit of the privileged classes, who applaud from their balconies.... once the battle has ended, of course. The booklet, which contains these beautiful theories of representative government, appeared on November 20; Lyon answered on the 21st. The response of the *Lyonnais* appeared so swiftly, that nobody said another word of the work of this propagandist.

What devastation the events of Lyon have just revealed to our eyes! The whole country was moved by pity at the sight of this army of spectra, half consumed by hunger, running into the grapeshot to die at least in one fell swoop.

And it is not only in Lyon; it is everywhere that the workmen die crushed by taxes. These men, once proud at the moment of the victory which marked their arrival onto the political scene and the triumph of freedom; these men who brought about the regeneration of all Europe, they struggle against hunger, a hunger does not leave them even enough strength to protest at each new dishonor added to the dishonor of the Restoration. Even the cry of dying Poland could not divert them from contemplation of their own miseries, and they kept what remains to them of their tears to cry over their lot and that of their children. What sufferings could make such people so quickly forget the exterminated Poles!

Here is the France of July as the ultra-royalists have given it to us. Who would have imagined it! In those intoxicating days, as we wandered automatically, rifle on shoulder, through unpaved streets and barricades, quite heedless of our triumph, our chests inflated with happiness, dreaming about the pale faces of the royalty and the joy of the people as the far-off roar of our singing of the *Marseillaise* would reach their ears; who would have imagined that such joy and glory would change into such mourning! Who would have thought, seeing these great six-foot tall workmen, before whom the bourgeoisie were left trembling their cellars, trembling, kissing their rags, and speaking again of their disinterestedness and their courage with sobs of admiration, who would have thought that they would die of poverty on these streets, of their being conquered, and that their former admirers would now call them the plague society!

Magnanimous spirits! Glorious workmen, whose dying hand my hand grasped in final adieu on the battle field, where I veiled the faces of the dying with rags, you died happy in the victory which was to redeem your race; and, six months later, I found your children lying in dungeons, and each evening I fell asleep on my bunk, with the noise of their moaning, the curses of their torturers, and the whistle of the whip which obscured their cries.

Is there not, dear sirs, some imprudence in lavishing these insults cast at men who withstood the test of their strength, and who suffer under conditions worse than those which pushed them into battle? Is it wise to teach the people such a bitter lesson how easily it was deceived by their moderation in triumph? Are you so certain that you will not need the clemency of the workers, that you can with full safety expose yourself to finding them pitiless? It seems that you take no other precautions against popular revenge than exaggerate the picture in advance, as if this exaggeration, these imaginary scenes of murder and plunder were the only means of forestalling their reality. It is easy to put the bayonet and grapeshot into men who surrendered their arms after the victory.

What will be less easy is to erase the memory of this victory. Almost eighteen months have been spent rebuilding bit by bit what was undone in forty-eight hours, and the eighteen months of reaction did not even shake the work of three days. No human power could eradicate that which was achieved. Ask of those who complained of an effect without a cause, if he flatters himself that there can be causes without effects. France conceived in the bloody embraces of six thousand heroes; childbirth can be long and painful; but the wombs are robust, and the ultra-royalist poisoners will not cause it to abort.

You confiscated the rifles of July. Yes; but the bullets have taken off. Every bullet of the Parisian workers is on its way around the world: they strike without cease; they will continue to strike until not a single enemy of the happiness of the people and of freedom is left standing.

Democratic Propaganda

Citizen:

The sympathies of the masses, tempered anew by a system of terror, are reawakening more lively than ever. They are a spring that compression has made more energetic and that only asks to be released. It is up to us to favor this movement of expansion. If the *doctrinaires* were able to flatter themselves that they had crushed democracy with no chance of return it's because the late catastrophe permitted them to put a halt to propaganda.

Re-establish it and we will move forward.

For the aristocracy is powerless to fight against republicans on the field of ideas. If the press is still an arm in its hands it's because it uses it to spread slander while we, with the sole force of our doctrines of equality and fraternity, are sure to carry the masses along.

But it's necessary that our voice reach them.

Let us then unite our efforts, citizen, in order to destroy the most odious of monopolies, the monopoly on enlightenment. Let us prove to the proletarians that that they have the right to ease with freedom; to free, common and equal education; to intervene in the government, all of which are forbidden them.

As you see, citizen, we have less a political change in mind than a social re-foundation. The extension of political rights, electoral reform, and universal suffrage can be excellent things, but only as means, not as goals. What our goal is is the equal sharing of the charges and benefits of society, is the total establishment of the reign of equality. Without this radical reorganization all formal modifications in government will be nothing but lies, all revolutions nothing but comedies performed for the benefit of the ambitious.

But it isn't enough to vaguely declare that all men are equal; it's not enough to combat the slanders of the evil, to destroy prejudices, and the habits of servility carefully maintained among the people. Through principles it's necessary to replace the prejudices in their hearts. It's necessary to convince the proletarians that equality is possible, that it is necessary. They must be penetrated with the sentiment of their dignity and clearly shown their rights and duties.

This must be the direction of our efforts. They will only be effective with the cooperation of all republicans: we appeal to their devotion and ask for their active and disinterested cooperation.

It is evident that new writings with the goal we have just indicated from a republican pen would be the object of perpetual harassment, whatever their moderation. We have resolved to foil the zeal of the police. What is important to us above all is to enlighten the masses. Trials, imprisonments and fines would quickly smash our efforts, despite all of our patriotically inspired perseverance.

We will limit ourselves to propagandizing by reprinting fragments of the best works published in the interests of the people, works that have freely circulated for some time.

We will select those that most clearly deal with the great questions of EQUALITY AND LIBERTY.

Those that tend to establish as the sole basis for social institutions the principle of the BROTHERHOOD of man and as sole guarantee of their lasting quality the *responsibility* of power.

If the ideas developed by these diverse writings are not always as up to date as those most advanced in their interest in the future might hope, it should be remembered that public instruction is in such a sad state that those truths that are old for the enlightened are new to the proletarian.

The writings we will publish will have four in-12 pages

and will appear irregularly in such a way as to form a brochure of ninety-six pages at the end of the year.

For 1 fr. 25 c. 100 copies will be received at home.

It is possible to subscribe for a smaller number.

Those citizens in Paris and the departments who want to second us in these efforts are requested to send their exact names and addresses to Rouanet's bookstore, Rue Verdelet, no. 6

L-Auguste Blanqui, Hadot-Desages

Our publications will appear irregularly, twice a month.

Since most writings cannot reach the people, who don't have the means to pay for them, the particular goal that we have proposed is to remedy this situation by a free distribution to proletarians. Those citizens who want to second us in our work should spread among the people the copies they have received buy giving them out.

In order to receive the publications at home it is necessary to subscribe for twenty copies of each publication, postage costs not permitting us to send fewer than this. Subscribers for fewer than twenty copies must get them at the office, Rouanet's , Rue Verdelet, No 6.

Organization of the Society of Families

Each fraction of the society is called a family.

The family is made up of five initiated, who meet twice a month under the presidency of a chief named by the center.

In order to be admitted one must be of age, have a good reputation and good conduct, justify one's means of existence, and be gifted with great discretion.

Proposals for membership are made within the family, which discusses the merits of the candidate and can refuse or accept him.

The names, estate, and lodging of the candidate are immediately sent to the center so that scrupulous investigation can be made concerning the morality, sobriety, discretion and energy of the candidate.

No opening should be made before this information is addressed to the chief of the family.

If the opening is accepted the presenter turns over to the candidate a series of questions that he must answer prior to his reception.

Receptions are made blindfolded by the chief of the family, in the presence of the proposed member alone.

In so far as it is possible, they must take place during the day and, in any event, in the light.

The chief of the family must never forget to say to the recipient that no trace remains of what is done, that it is impossible for the police to discover anything, and that consequently no confession must ever be made in court, under penalty of passing for a traitor and being punished as such.

The recipient must be made to feel the importance of entering the National Guard.

Questions should be posed on arms and munitions.

The work is directed by the chief of the family who, at the opening of sessions, makes a report on what transpired at the previous session.

The work is terminated by proposals, presentations, and the collecting of dues.

First issue of "Le Libérateur"

Goal of the newspaper

Of all the exclusions that weigh on the citizen without a fortune, the most painful and the one most bitterly felt is that which prohibits him from publishing his thoughts. One can be consoled for not participating in the election of a deputy or a municipal functionary. But we are profoundly wounded by the evil designs of a legislation that restricts thought when that thought doesn't have the insolent pass handed out by wealth. Those men devoted to defending the principle of equality will never forgive the ministers whose popular names served as a cloak for that law of security deposits and franking that makes the press a slave to the opulent classes, for it is they who bear the responsibility for that irreparable fault. And when, carried away by the boiling up of indignation against triumphant iniquity they raise their voices, an iron glove smashes the words on their lips. They are forbidden to take in hand the interests of the oppressed: they don't have the right to that. It's a right that only belongs to the rich; one must be rich in order to better identify with the poor, and riches alone gives the guts to feel and express their sufferings.

This newspaper is a protest against force's insulting derision. A lone citizen, without money, without a *sou* put away, undertakes to brave the prohibition imposed by the aristocracy of the *ecu* against the poor man who dares to think. With his health destroyed, barely out of the prison where a verdict had him expiate the cries he raised up in favor of exploited workers, his hands still marked by the imprint of handcuffs, he today again takes up arms. And he will write, having ceaselessly before his eyes the unfortunate brothers that he left behind in those sad tombs. He is not one of those men who, in the midst of a society torn apart by passions, claims to feel no passion; who in order not to displease selfish dominators protects himself against all convictions as if they were evil things, and affects to maintain a cowardly impartiality between those who suffer and those who cause suffering. The only role appropriate for an honest man is that of loudly avowing his affections and his hatreds. One should feel sorry for those who boast of the fact that they neither love nor hate anyone, for if they are telling the truth they have nothing in their breasts. And if they lie, what authority remains to their words?

Those of *Le Liberateur* will be frank, with neither reticence nor hesitations. On one hand it will make an effort to expose in simple, clear, and precise terms why the people are unhappy and how they can cease to be so. It will explain the nature of the relationships that exist today between the master and the worker, the social question that virtually on its own constitutes all of political economy, and about which professors say barely a word. And at the same time, addressing itself to men whose profound meditations turn them from the hustle and bustle of the moment in order to embrace from on high all of humanity in its past and its future, it will submit to them its critical views on the current organization, or rather, disorganization, as well as ideas on the principles that should preside over the re-composition of the social order.

Who Makes the Soup Should Eat It

Wealth is born of intelligence and labor. But these two forces can only act with the aid of a passive element – the land, which they put to work by their combined efforts. It thus seems that this indispensable instrument should belong to all men. Such is not the case.

Individuals have taken over common land by ruse or violence, declaring themselves its owners; they have established by law that it will always be theirs, and that the right to property will become the foundation of the social constitution; which is to say that it will come before and, if need be, absorb all human rights, even that to life, if it has the ill fortune to find itself in conflict with the privilege of a small number.

The right to property has extended itself by logical deduction from the land to other instruments: the accumulated products of labor, designated by the generic name of capital. Since capital, sterile in and of itself can only fructify through labor, and , on the other hand, since it is the primary matter worked on by social forces, the majority, excluded from its possession, finds itself condemned to forced labor, to the profit of the possessing minority. Neither the instruments nor the fruits of labor belong to the workers, but to the idlers. The gluttonous branches absorb the tree's sap, to the detriment of the fertile boughs. The hornets devour the honey created by the bees.

Such is our social order, founded on conquest, which has divided populations into victors and vanquished. The logical consequence of such an organization is slavery. And we didn't have to wait long for its arrival. In fact, with land acquiring value only from cultivation, the privileged have drawn the conclusion that, thanks to the right to own land, they also have that to own the human livestock that makes it fertile. In the first place they have considered it as a complement to their domain but, in the final analysis, they see it as personal property, independent of the land.

Nevertheless, the principle of equality, engraved in the depths of the heart, and which conspires, with the centuries, to destroy the exploitation of man by man in all its forms, delivered the first blow to the sacrilegious right to property by smashing slavery. Privilege was forced to reduce itself to the possession of men not as furniture, but as real estate auxiliary to, and inseparable from, real estate in the form of land.

In the 16th century a deadly rebirth of oppression brought about the enslavement of blacks; and even today the inhabitants of a land reputed to be French own men in the same way as clothing and horses. There is, in fact, less of a difference than meets the eye between our state and that of the colonies. After eighteen centuries of war between privilege and equality the homeland, theatre and principal champion of this struggle, could not put up with slavery in its naked brutality. But the fact exists in name, and the right to property, while more hypocritical in Paris than in Martinique, is neither less inflexible nor less oppressive.

In fact, servitude does not consist solely in being a man's thing, or a lord's serf. He is not free who, deprived of the instruments of labor, remains at the mercy of the privileged who are their owners. This is the state that feeds revolt. In order to exorcise this peril they try to reconcile Cain with Abel. From the necessity of capital as an instrument of labor they go on to conclude in the community of interests, and then to that of solidarity between the capitalist and the worker. How many artistically embroidered phrases there are on this canvas! The lamb is shorn for his own health. It owes thanks. Our Aesculapiuses know how to sugar-coat the pill.

There are still some who are fooled by these homilies, but they are few. Each day the light shines brighter on this so-called association of the parasite and its victim. But the facts are eloquent; they prove the duel, the duel to the death, between revenue and salary. It's a question of justice and good sense. Let's examine the situation.

There is no society without labor! What's more, there exist no idlers who do not have need of workers. But what need do workers have of idlers? Is capital only productive in the workers' hands on condition that it not belong to them? I imagine the proletariat, deserting *en masse,* taking its tools and its labor to some distant land. Would it by chance die due to the absence of its masters? Can the new society only come about by creating lords of the land and of capital, in handing over to a caste of idlers the ownership of all the instruments of labor? Is there no other social mechanism possible but this division of owners and the salaried?

On the other hand, how curious it would be to see the expression on the faces of our proud lords abandoned by their slaves. What would be done with their palaces, their workshops, their deserted fields? Would they die of hunger in the midst of their riches, or would they put on work clothes, take up the pick and, in their turn, humbly sweat on some plot of land? How much would all of them cultivate?

But a people of 32 million souls doesn't retire to Mount Aventine. Let us then take the opposite and more realizable hypothesis. One fine day the idlers evacuate the soil of France, which remains in the workers' hands. A day of happiness and triumph! What an immense relief for so many chests, relieved of the weight that crushes them! How freely this multitude breathes. Citizens – sing in chorus the song of deliverance!

Axiom: the nation is impoverished by the death of a worker. She is enriched by that of an idler. The death of a wealthy man is a benefit.

Yes! The right of property is in decline. Generous spirits prophesy and call for its fall. The Essenian principle of reality has slowly sapped it over the course of eighteen centuries through the successive abolition of the various servitudes which served as the basis for its power. It will disappear one day, along with the last privileges that serve as its refuge and nook. The past and the present guarantee us this resolution. For humanity is never stationary. It either advances or goes back. Its progressive march led it to equality. Its backward march climbs, by all of privilege's steps, to personal slavery, the final word in the right of property. To be sure, before returning there, European civilization would have perished. But through what catastrophe? A Russian invasion? To the contrary, it is the north that will itself be invaded by the principle of equality that the French bring in the conquest of nations. The future is not in doubt.

Let us immediately say that equality doesn't consist in the partitioning of land. The splitting up of land will really change nothing concerning the right of property. With wealth growing from the ownership of the instruments of labor, rather than through labor itself, the spirit of exploitation left standing would soon know, through the reconstruction of large fortunes, how to restore social inequality.

Association alone, in place of private property, will serve as the basis for the reign of justice through equality. This is the foundation of the growing ardor of men of the future to make clear and highlight the elements of association. We, too, will perhaps bring our contingent to the common task.

Appeal of the Committee of the Society of the Seasons

To arms, Citizens!

The fatal hour has rung for the oppressors.

The cowardly tyrant of the Tuileries laughs at the hunger that tears at the guts of the people. But the measure of his crimes is full. They are finally going to receive their punishment.

Betrayed France, the blood of our murdered brothers cry out to you and demand vengeance. Let it be terrible, for it has delayed too long. Let exploitation perish, and may equality triumphantly assume its seat on the intermingled debris of royalty and aristocracy.

The provisional government has chosen military chiefs for the guiding of the combat. These chiefs come from your ranks. Follow them! They will lead you to victory.

Their names are:

Auguste Blanqui, Commander-in-Chief; Barbés, Martin-Bernard, Quignot, Meillard, Nétré, Divisional Commanders of the Republican Army.

Arise, People, and your enemies will disappear like dust before a hurricane! Strike, exterminate without pity the vile henchmen, tyranny's voluntary accomplices. But extend your hand to those soldiers who come from your midst and who will never turn their parricidal arms against you.

57

Forward! Vive la République!

The members of the Provisional Government:
Barbés, Voyer d'Argenson, Auguste Blanqui, Lamennais, Martin-Bernard, Dubosc, Laponeraye.

Paris, May 12, 1839

Address of Central Republican Society to the Government

We have the firm hope that the government issued from the barricades of 1848 will not, like its predecessor, want to put back in place, along with each paving stone, a law of repression. With this in mind, we offer our assistance to the Provisional Government in the realization of the (beautiful) motto: *Liberté, Egalité, Fraternité.*

We that demand that the government (immediately) decree as a result of the popular victory:

1. The complete and unlimited freedom of the press.
2. The absolute and irrevocable suppression of security deposits and franking and postal rights [for the press].
3. The complete freedom of circulation for works of the intellect through all possible means: through posters, peddlers, public criers, without any restrictions or hindrances, without any need for prior authorization.
4. The freedom of the printing industry and the suppression of all privileges represented by licenses, though with prior indemnification.
5. The holding blameless of printers for any writing whose author is known.
6. The suppression of art. 291 of the Penal Code, of the law of April 9 1834, and the formal abrogation of laws, ordinances, decrees, edicts or rules of any kind, dated previous to February 25, 1848, capable of limiting or inhibiting the absolute and inalienable right to association and gathering.
7. The removal from the standing and sitting magistracy of those from the three last reigns, and their provisional replacement by lawyers, advocates, notaries, etc.
8. The immediate armament and organization in National Guards of all workers not established in a profession and

who receive a salary, without any exception, with an indemnity of two francs for each day of active service.

9. The abrogation of art. 415 and 416 of the Penal Code, as well as of all special laws against working-class coalitions.

Central Republican Society to the Provisional Government

Citizens:

The counter-revolution has just bathed in the blood of the people. Judgment, immediate judgment of the assassins!

For the past two months the royalist bourgeoisie of Rouen has plotted in the shadows a St Bartholomew's massacre of the workers. It had stocked up on cartridges. The authorities knew of this.

Calls for death had broken out here and there, the premonitory symptoms of the catastrophe. *We have to have done with these scoundrels!* Scoundrels who in February, after three days of resistance, forced the bourgeois guard to submit to the Republic.

Citizens of the Provisional Government, how is it that in two months the working class population of Rouen and the surrounding valleys were not organized into National Guard units?

How is it that only the aristocracy possessed organization and arms?

How is it that at the moment of the execution of its horrible plot it only met unarmed breasts?

How is it that the 28th Regiment of the line, this sinister hero of the *faubourg de Vaise*, was in Rouen?

How is it that the garrison obeyed the orders of generals who were declared enemies of the Republic, of a General Gerard, creature and henchman of Louis-Philippe?

They were thirsty for a bloody revenge, these hired killers

of a fallen dynasty. They needed an April massacre as consolation for a second July. They didn't have to wait long.

April days barely two months after the revolution!

And nothing was missing from these new April scenes! Neither guns, nor bullets nor destroyed houses, nor state of siege nor the ferocity of the soldiers, nor the insulting of the dead, nor the unanimous insults from the newspapers, these cowardly adorers or might. The rue Transnonain has been surpassed. Upon reading the wretched story of the exploits of these brigands we again find ourselves in the aftermath of the horrible days that once covered France in mourning and shame.

These are exactly the same executioners and the same victims! On one side frenzied bourgeois pushing to carnage imbecilic soldiers that they have filled with wine and hatred. On the other unfortunate workers defenselessly falling under the bullets and bayonets of the assassins.

And as a final sign of resemblance, here comes the royal court, Louis-Philippe's judges, falling like hyenas on the debris of the massacre and filling the prisons with 250 republicans. At the head of these inquisitors is Frank-Carré, the execrable *procureur-general* of the court of peers, this Laubardemont who asked with rage for the heads of the insurgents of May 1839. The arrest warrants followed those patriots to Paris who fled the royalist proscription.

For it is a royalist terror that reigns in Rouen: do you not know this citizens of the Provisional Government? The bourgeois guard of Rouen furiously rejected the Republic in February. It is the Republic that it blasphemes and that it wants to overthrow.

All that was Republican yesterday has been put in irons. Your very own agents have been threatened with death, removed from office, arrested. The municipal magistrates Lemason and Durand have been dragged through the streets, bayonets at their chests, their clothing in rags. They are being held in secret by authority of the rebels. It is a royalist insurrection that has triumphed in the ancient capital of Normandy, and it is you, republican government, that supports these rebel assassins! Is this treason or is this cowardice? Are you weaklings or accomplices?

You know full well that there was no battle: it was a slaughter! And you let the slaughterers recount their feats of prowess! Is it that in your eyes, like in those of kings, the blood of the people is nothing but water, good for washing down the over-encumbered streets from time to time? If so, then erase from your buildings that detestable lie in three words that you have just inscribed on them: Liberty, Equality, Fraternity!

If your wives, if your daughters, those brilliant and frail creatures who promenade their idleness in gold and silk in sumptuous equipages, had been thrown at your feet, their breast opened by the fire of pitiless enemies, what cries of pain and vengeance you'd make heard to the ends of the earth!

So go, go see stretched out on the slabs of your hospitals, on cots in mansards these cadavers of slaughtered women, their breasts perforated by bourgeois bullets; the very breast that bore and nourished the workers whose sweat fattens the bourgeois!

The women of the people are worth as much as yours, and their blood should not, cannot remain unavenged!

Justice, then, justice for the assassins!

We demand:

1. The dissolution and disarmament of the bourgeois guard of Rouen
2. The arrest and trial of the generals and officers of the Bourgeois Guard and the troops of the line who ordered and led the massacre
3. The arrest and trial of the so-called members of the court of appeals, henchmen named by Louis-Philippe who,

acting in the name and for the account of the victorious royalist faction, imprisoned the legitimate magistrates of the city and filled the prisons with republicans

4. Sending far from Paris the troops of the line who at this very moment, at fratricidal banquets, the reactionaries are readying for a St Bartholomew's massacre of Parisian workers.

For the Central Republican Society, the members of the Bureau:

L-Auguste Blanqui, chairman
C.Lacambre,DMO – Vice-Chair
Flotte, treasurer
Pierre Beraud, Loroue secretaries, members of the Bureau
G. Robert
Lachambeaude
Crousse
Pujol
Javelot jeune
Brucker
Fomberteaux

To The Democratic Clubs of Paris

The Republic would be a lie if it were to be only the substitution of one form of government for another. It's not enough to change words: things must be changed.

The Republic means the emancipation of workers, it's the end of the reign of exploitation, it's the coming of a new order that will free labor from the tyranny of capital.

Liberté! Égalité! Fraternité! This motto that shone from the front of our buildings should not be a vain opera decoration.

No silly baubles! We are no longer children. There is no freedom where there is no bread. There is no equality when opulence scandalously exists alongside poverty. There is no brotherhood when the worker drags himself to the door of palaces with his starving children.

Work and bread! The existence of the people cannot remain at the mercy of the fears and the rancor of capital.

Those popular societies that share our principles are invited to select three delegates who will meet at the central electoral committee, Sunday March 26 at 11:00 am in the Conference room, rue des Poiriers, near the Sorbonne. Only delegates from clubs will be admitted and should have with them the powers granted them by their respective societies.

Parisians!

If there is still time, open your eyes at the polling booth to the peril that threatens you: Paris is condemned and its sentence is being carried out by the hands of a reaction that was able to everywhere recruit accomplices in and instruments of its vengeance.

Under the pretext of disencumberment, of public order and even of humanity, every day the capital is being emptied of the working class. A fatal measure! A death measure!

With the exception of a small handful of rich idlers the entire city only lives only thanks to the workers: without workers there is no more consumption, and thus no more business! The mass of retailers would fall into ruin, big business and industry would follow them into the abyss, and the faction that represents the victorious past would applaud the ruin of this Paris that it abhors because it has changed the face of the world.

Merchants, landlords, don't second these evil designs; leave behind your terrors and fears. What do the people ask for? To live in happiness through their labor, and interest orders you to support this just demand, for your profits come from the people, you earn them as a result of their consumption. Don't let appearances fool you! In the ocean of affairs, spending on luxury items is but a drop of water. For every person who lives off the gold of the rich nine live on the *centimes* of the poor. Between you and the workers there is solidarity.

But be just! The people have suffered for too long! They no longer can nor will suffer under the harsh conditions made for them by the rapacity of the moneyed. They ask for a more equitable ones, and it is this demand that is rejected with violence, with fury...They persist, they claim to drive them to ask for mercy, they are hunted down through famine...But they don't surrender! They will advance, shaking the dust from their feet.

Their property doesn't tie them down them, and they are already leaving. And Paris, without any people, will enter its agony.

When the grass grows green between the cobblestones it will be too late for you merchants without business and landlords without rent to cry in the doorways of your closed up shops and your deserted houses! You will have order just as in Milan or Warsaw, and you will perhaps find that the rolling of cannons on the streets is not worth as much as that of trucks and carts.

There remains one chance for salvation: that you freely join the people in order to ensure that they receive what they ask for, i.e., *well-paid* work and, above all else, the choice of representatives who will want to accomplish these tasks *without any delay and at whatever cost*, carry out this task.

It isn't enormous; it suffices to not remain prostrated before capital and to render them that good will they showed for an instant after the events of February. Above all, don't forget that your mortal enemy is provincial reaction. You know where to find it, for it doesn't hide itself.

With its saber high it is leading the charge on Paris. Remember the sinister phrase of Isnard, a representative of one of the small towns: "If Paris dares attack national sovereignty travelers will soon search the banks of the Seine in an attempt to find the place on which Paris stood."

This phrase is the key to the situation. Isnard and his ilk wanted to suffocate the great city in the hothouse of the army, and history is there to show us that their triumph would have ended with the carving up of France. They failed, and the holy city made of us the first people in the world.

Paris, the capital of intelligence and labor, is the true national representative body, the gigantic and majestic congress where the whole country, through the elite of its united children – writers, artists, workers, scientists, industrialists – is ceaselessly occupied in making shine the labor of its grandeur and prosperity.

68

Reaction aims to paralyze the nation by cutting off its brain. Parisians! It's up to you, rich and poor, to prevent France from being decapitated and to hold back the hand that the parricides raise against their mothers!

Think of this at the polling booth.

Auguste Blanqui
Dungeon of Vincennes
September 15, 1848

Blanqui's Response to the Tascherau Document

Suddenly a strange piece has appeared in an unknown journal. It accuses the principal leader of the secret societies between 1834-39 of treason.

Blanqui, the supposed author, did not write it, didn't sign it. No sign reveals its origin or guarantees its authenticity.

It's a question here of killing a man who had become an obstacle and a danger. Using police and court clerk notes, perhaps even using personal memories, a history of the secret societies of the years 1835-39 was fabricated, and at the top was written: "Blanqui's Declaration before the Minister of the Interior."

And so here I am garbed in the shirt of Nessus!

What was the forger's secret? The use of the first person. How can anyone resist the magical influence of the words *I, me* that are repeatedly used in the tale as the personification of the same man? It's him! They cry: he speaks, he tells all, he's on stage.

It is forgotten that for thirty years, using the same method, and using the notes of chambermaids, literary fabricators have constructed heaps of so-called historical memoirs in the name of every possible person. I cite those of Napoleon published in 1820. The illusion was universal and people barely gave credence to the still living Napoleon's denial. What was the procedure of the Abbot Pradt, the author of the mystification? A strong style and direct speech.

In the document in the *Revue Retrospective* replace the pronouns *I* and *me* with *Blanqui* and what is left? An incomplete and irregular account of the secret societies that is of impenetrable paternity. Even more. Substitute the words *I* and *me* for every name cited in the piece, suppressing the portrait of the author they make speak, and you will find the same revelation successively made by these various people.

It's in my style, they say. Take my entire literary baggage: it's quite thin. Let a jury of writers compare the factum with it and if he finds the least analogy with my style then I stand condemned.

And if it's not my style, it's even less my writing. Maybe you dictated it. No! In several places in this piece there is a certain care shown in the style, which doesn't allow for the improvisation of the dictated word. I had to have written it. Where is the manuscript? I was a prisoner. I couldn't take it out and they had a capital interest in possessing it.

No signature either! Is this believable? How could this be? Here was an old, dangerous enemy at their mercy, prostrated at the feet of the victors, handing over his past, his person, and they didn't take the least guarantee, the least pledge, not even his simple signature!

And the very next day this coward stands up to his full height before the Court of Peers! He braves the judges with his words! With his silence! In the middle of the courtroom he justifies his insurrection! He publicly humiliates those whose knees he embraced the day before! How does this excess of cowardice on October 22, far from danger, gibe with the excess of daring on January 14, in the very presence of danger?

Slander is always welcome. Hatred and credulity savor it with joy. It doesn't have to dress itself up; as long as it kills, what difference does verisimilitude make? Even absurdity doesn't do it harm. It has a secret advocate in every heart: envy. It is never asked for explanations or proofs: rather its victims are. An entire life of devotion, austerity and suffering are destroyed in a second with a wave of its hand.

Treason! But why? To save my head which, as everyone knows, wasn't threatened? If the scaffold couldn't be built when vengeance was at its highest point, could it be raised after eight months of pacification and forgetting? It would at least have been necessary to await its presence. And if an excess of terror so hastily forced me into being an informer how, I ask again, did they not wrench a signature from that moral annihilation?

Did I at least manage to lighten my irons? Mont Saint Michel and the penitentiary at Tours answer this question. Who among my companions has drunk as deeply as me from the cup of anguish? For a year the death agony of a beloved wife, dying far from me in despair, and then four whole years, an eternal tête-à-tête in the solitude of a cell, with the ghost of she who was no more. This was my torture, mine alone, and now I hear ringing in my ears: Death to the traitor! Crucify him!

"You sold your brothers for a good price!" writes the prostituted pen of the orgiasts. Gold so I could go and slowly die in a tomb, between black bread and the pitcher of anguish. And what did I do with this gold? I live in an attic with fifty centimes a day. For entire fortune at present I have sixty francs. And yet it's me, a sad wretch who drags his wounded body in rags through the streets, who is attacked with the name of sell-out while Louis-Philippe's valets have metamorphosed into brilliant republican butterflies, fluttering around the carpets of the Hotel de Ville, from the heights of their well nourished virtue branding the poor Job who escaped from the prisons of their master.

Oh sons of man, who forever hold in your hands a stone to throw at the innocent, contempt be upon you!

The most benevolent say: "This must be some letter, some note of Blanqui's perfidiously transformed into a denunciation." They vaguely suspect an evil deed, without putting the evidence's paternity in question. Two things fascinate them: the use of the first person, so powerful in encouraging illusions, and the sudden revelation of this underground world of secret societies.

Good people, don't be fooled. Not a word of this writing is from my pen. It comes in its entirety from the filthy laboratory of the forgers.

These facts, so new to you, so strange, for the past nine years have been of the domain of publicity, emanating from a circle that includes no less than 1500 people. Among the oldest members of the *Families* and the *Seasons* there has been but one cry: "We know all this for a long time; there are at least a hundred of us that could have written this note." And in fact it is nothing but a short, incomplete excerpt from among the countless files the police have on the matter. As for the portraits sketched out in this lampoon the artisan had an embarrassment of riches among the full face, three quarter, and profiles that the cartons furnished on all the principal and secondary characters. The police had the time and the millions needed to put together this collection, not counting what our internecine quarrels provided them gratis.

For the rest, this so-called revelation is not a revelation; it's a vagabond stroll through the history of the four preceding years. What did the confiding of a thousand stories better known to him than anyone matter to the minister? What was the use of these details that had long since fallen into the dust of the court clerks? Written by hand this piece is conceivable; dictated it is impossible. We accept a manuscript is such as it is, but they would have said to a blabbermouth: "Let's move on to the subject of the Flood and talk about something else."

In this endless mass there aren't twenty lines of revelations. They have to do with the personnel of the Society of the Seasons, reconstituted after May 12. Two men could be found in the new committee: a direct leader of half the society members, who was later recognized to be a police agent, and the other, a man of intelligence and knowledge, who became a royal procurator.

Let's not forget the spy Teissier, friend and confidant of Lamieussens; Delahodde, member of the *Family* and the *Seasons,* living closely with the principal leaders. Here were sufficient sources of information for the rue de Jerusalem.

In summary, nine tenths of the lampoon is nothing but a series of useless divagations. As a denunciation it is an absurdity. But in the hypothesis of a fraud this grand historical exposé is indispensable for displaying the man they want to destroy and to portray his personality in a series of gripping details.

Another observation: there are strange disparities of language among the various parts of this document. Here animated developments, there absolute nudity. What is the source of these sudden changes from a picturesque style to that of an inventory? These contradictions, inexplicable in a narrator who allows his pen or his voice to flow with his thoughts become quite simple in a work fabricated of pieces and morsels.

If the piece is true it reveals an unreserved abandon, a decision to tell everything. What is more, my memories were recent and complete, so I couldn't err or mislead others. Yet this document is full of errors, of nonsense, of contradictions and absurdities. This being so, how can it be attributed to me?

So I am made to say:

1. That I created the Society of Families in June 1835. *It was founded by Hadot-Desages and I only entered it later.*
2. That its prescribed effectives were about 750 men. Completely false. *The number was unlimited.*
3. That there never existed a list of society members accepted, only those presented. *Another error. Both existed.*
4. That May 12, 650 Society members gathered, and four lines later 850 presented themselves. *A flagrant contradiction, impossible in the space of half a minute.*
5. That on the day of combat we possessed 3000 cartridges. *We had 10,000; I knew the exact number.*
6. That the majority of well-dressed republicans produce

75

newspapers. *This is quite a strange statistic.*
7. That we hadn't in advance designated the members of a Provisional Government. *The printed proclamation containing the list of names of the members of this government was the main evidence in out trial at the Court of Peers.*
8. That Nettré was killed in May. *Nettré is alive; I knew him to be in England and in good health before my arrest, etc.*

I am made to speak of M. Emmanuel Arago, who I never saw, who I didn't know at all; of Vilcoq, about whom I had always held an opinion diametrically opposed to the one they put in my mouth.

Without pausing any longer over details, I will say that all these errors, impossible on my part, are only explicable in the case of a forgery. The arranger worked on a pile of dossiers and reports; all that was needed was an imprecise misunderstood, or incorrectly filed note to create an error, a blunder, nonsense. All the falsehoods I revealed above certainly had their origin in this.

What is more, the miserable fabricator wasn't able to carry this out to the end without betraying himself. The third part of the document is nothing but a confused mess of bits and pieces without order or meaning, a tissue of notes tied sewed together any which way and deprived of any meaning. The worker stumbles at every step and ends up being caught in his own trap. He forgets that I am on stage, that I speak, and in the middle of my speech he suddenly places a police note directed against me.

Here, the note says, is Blanqui's escape plan: "He had accepted to reorganize the Society, but he wanted to leave once the organization was set up. He proposed going to Switzerland. After two or three months he lost all direction. We would no longer be forced to ask from him our marching orders."

So it is I who speak in this way about myself! The Homer

of this marvelous Iliad had doubtless fallen asleep at the moment of this heavy fall. *Quandunque bonus dormitat Homerus.* The wretch didn't see that he cast into my harangue, and as a part of my harangue, the report of the spy who handed me over to the enemy when I left for Switzerland.

A strange, providential mistake that pinned the crime to the forger's hand for the greater edification of all.

I've finished with slander, let us now pass to the slanderers. It is time to confront them. This pamphlet, their master blow, wasn't their first attempt, for their hatred is fifteen years old.

The moment for public explanations has arrived. It sounded with the tocsin of February. We must finally bring into broad daylight these quarrels that have for so long simmered in the shadows.

My portrait doesn't have the honor of figuring in the gallery that a charitable hand has just extracted from the museums of the police. In order to fill in this lacuna I give it here, such as I know it, twenty times traced by my open enemies of today, my hidden enemies of the past.

"Somber spirit, haughty, ferocious, bad tempered, sarcastic, immense ambition, cold, inexorable, pitilessly crushing men in order to pave his route, heart of marble, head of iron, etc"

This profile isn't lovely. But is there no shading to this painting, and is the cry of hatred the gospel? I call on those who knew my domestic hearth. They know whether all my existence wasn't concentrated in a deep, lively affection where my forces were ever and again tempered for political struggles.

Death, in smashing this affection, stroke the sole blow, I confess, that could touch my soul. All the rest, slander included, slides off me like a dust storm. I shake off my clothes and I continue on my way.

Sycophants, you who want to put me forward as a moral monster, open the doors to your hearth and home, put your heart's life on display. Under your hypocritical exterior what would we find? The brutality of the senses, the perversity of the soul. Whited sepulchers, I lift the stone that hides your rot from people's eyes.

What you pursue in me is revolutionary inflexibility and stubborn devotion to ideas. You want to strike down the indefatigable fighter. What have you done for the past fourteen years? Defect. I was at the breach in 1831 with you; I was there with you in 1839, in 1847. In 1848 here I am against you.

May 12 willed me your hatred as a legacy. The affront of May 12 still burns your cheeks. To believe oneself the republic and not know that the republic gives battle. How forgive the daring sweep of a tail that made your impotence the subject of public laughter. The entire party remembers your rage and insults against the vanquished insurrection. *Le National* every morning bandaged your wounds with bile and mud, and cowardly insinuations preceded the slanders that finally are bursting upon me, unleashed by vengeance.

During my agony at Mont Saint-Michel these resentments were dormant. A dying man is not fearsome, and with the rumors of my imminent death many quills were perhaps being sharpened for a magnificent funeral oration. But death has retreated and February has changed these quills into daggers.

I arrived the 24th, swept away by the joy of triumph. What an icy reception! One would think I was a ghost suddenly arisen before the new masters. Who are they looking at with that look of aversion and fright? I understand. It's the hated author of May 12, the clear-sighted and staunch patriot who can't be made an accomplice or a dupe, who won't allow the revolution to be stolen. But already the new program of the Hotel de Ville has been decided on:

Change in form but not in content. The edifice of

privilege, without a single stone less, with a few additional phrases and banners.

Exile to the Luxembourg awaits those who want more.

So on the 25th Citizen Recurt said to me, "You want to overthrow us?" "No, rather block the road behind you." And the fight broke out immediately, loyal and moderate on my side, perfidious and implacable on the other.

A thousand rumors are spread about. "He's mad! Sorrow and then joy have shaken his brain. He's ill; he's decomposing, he's going to die. He's bloodthirsty! He's demanding 100,000 heads."

These rumors spread around Paris and the departments. But up to this point still not a word of the great slander. M. de Lamartine, at the Hotel de Ville, addressed me with these words:

"It is persecution that makes for your martyrdom and your glory."

Such language is not used concerning an informer.

So once again you lied, sieur in saying that your odious piece, passed around the city since February 24, was in your hands on March 10; your hatred would not have allowed it to slumber for so long and wouldn't have waited until the 22nd to spread its poison. No, before the 17th you didn't go so far. Effort can always be measured by the force of an obstacle. I was yet but a hindrance, not yet a danger. The moment for extreme measures had not yet sounded. During this time speech became more venomous, the Central Republican Society attacked with vivacity power's retrograde demands. The reestablishment of the stamp, the maintenance of the former magistracy, the poor choice of commissioners, the disastrous decrees concerning the alienation of state lands, the anticipated quarterly payments each became in their turn the objects of energetic addresses, voted on my presentation. But our complaints bumped up uselessly against the disdain of bias and did nothing but attract anger, while reaction, supported by the majority in government, advanced rapidly. It was time to stop them. The adjournment of elections to the Constituent Assembly, twice demanded by the Republican Society, had been twice refused.

From March 12-16 at various assemblies of state bodies I proposed the support of the workers' demands en masse. The proposal was received with enthusiasm.

On the 17th at noon Paris was set in motion and 200,000 men surrounded the Hotel de Ville. At the sight of that living sea, in waves on the squares and quays, with a formidable clamor resistance falls, the retrograde faction disappeared. Everything was promised; everything was granted to the deputation that spoke in the name of the people.

An intrigue strived to falsify the meaning of this great demonstration and see in it nothing but a response to the National Guard's skirmish. Nothing could be more false. The popular movement had been stopped before the 16th, and its organizers were ignorant of the petty plot of the men in shakos. Chance alone was responsible for bringing together the execution of these two contrary efforts.

The events of the 17th struck the majority of the Provisional Government with terror; it thought it had escaped from a great danger. Absurd reports, and perhaps the awareness of its own sins persuaded it of the existence of plans for its overthrow, of armed violence.

Suspicion fell on me. I was the first, and almost the only one, to have raised the question of the adjournment of elections; I had kept it on the order of the day despite repeated failure, and finally that question had brought 200,000 men onto the public square.

Other influences, which had more collaborated in this great movement more than I, hid themselves before alerted eyes, fixed on one peril alone. It was thus the hostility of the moment, that which had to be smashed at whatever price. From this came two ideas that blossomed at almost the same time: one, that of modifying the government by my accession, the other, born of the fright caused by the first, to crush me with a club.

The entire reactionary faction trembled at the very threat that power was going to fall into the hands of the revolution, and in those lairs of Machiavellianism where the only crime is that of not succeeding a desperate plan was cooked up to ward off the peril and grab victory in hand.

Daring inspired the plotters. Without this determined coup, the popular party would today have been triumphant, reaction wiped out and the republic in full and vigorous march towards the realization of the future.

Look around us: the revolution is stumbling. The mass of its enemies is growing and increases from hour to hour. It is erupting through the breach I left open. I am conscious of this; I bore its flag. If it falls, the republic will follow.

It was I who had to be struck first, and numerous signs served as a prelude to the grand attack. March 19 the rumor spread with rapidity in the *faubourg* Saint-Antoine that I was a paid agent of the party of Henri V. Upon investigation it was recognized that these statements come from a rabble-rouser devoted to the Paris city hall. Three days later the decisive method was finally found.

And thus the plan for war to death developed. From the 17th to the 22nd the other idea, that of negotiation with the presumed leader of the movement, had also followed its course. The two plots unfurled in parallel.

On the 19th M. X. Durrieu, editor in chief of the *Courrier Francais* said to me: "M. de Lamartine wishes to come to an agreement with you. He recognizes that the government must be modified. He has decided to throw out the coterie of the *National* and to join with you and your friends. He will do whatever you wish; he'll go as far as you. I have been charged with bringing on his behalf words of reconciliation to Ledru-Rollin."

At first I refused this interview, and only ceded two days later to his repeated pleas. A meeting was set for the 22nd, but at the moment fixed M. X. Durrieu said to me, "It's not going to happen. Lamartine has changed his mind. He's made a complete turnabout. He thinks that everything is going fine, that the people are happy, and that things should continue as they are. That man is the very personification of changeability and inconsistency."

Fine. Let's not bother talking anymore.

And here is the source of the mystery: it's the 22nd that the famous piece makes its first appearance. That very day it is brought to the provisional Government. It is passed from hand to hand. Surprise! Exclamations! "Blanqui!" each reader repeats. "Blanqui!" But it's not his writing. The original must be at the Luxembourg someone says. They doubtless searched the Luxembourg. I'm still waiting for the original.

Let's return to the dates, since this is the whole trial. The piece appears at the Hotel de Ville the 22nd, not a day sooner. How then could the sieur claim that it was stolen on February 24 from M. Guizot's office, passed around for a week and put at his disposal around March 10. What? A document of such seriousness would have been passed everywhere from February 24 without anyone knowing about it? M., a close friend of the National, kept it in his wallet for twelve days without breathing a word to anyone and until the 22nd not a sound, not an echo betrayed its existence.

For I repeat: before the 22nd there was no trace of the lampoon.

That day it unexpectedly falls into the midst of several members of the Provisional Government. A coup de theatre and a coup d'etat. At that very instant everything changes. Reaction, almost defeated, raises its head. It appeared that a providential hand had just saved it from shipwreck. Confidence succeeds despair. M. de Lamartine breaks off his negotiations with the public agitator. He is less feared, and they no longer hesitate to falsify the word given to the people. The election isn't adjourned till the May 31; it was only deferred a few days due to material reasons.

What promptness in exploiting this document! It becomes known the 22nd and the 24th several provincial newspapers reproduce in the same terms the following note emanating from the offices of the *National.*

"We could name a certain club president, a fiery democrat who was miserable enough to betray the secrets of his political friends in order to save his own life. *The Provisional Government has many pieces of evidence in its hands* which are condemn those who want to undermine it as well as the social order that guides us so as to substitute for it a bloody chaos under the pretext of fraternity. It will remain disdainful and magnanimous *until the day it is forced to resort to reprisals.*"

And so by your own confession the publication of this cowardly lampoon is *nothing but a reprisal.* It isn't an act of justice, but an act of revenge. Your goal is *to condemn those who want to undermine you,* i.e., those who oppose you.

So again it isn't sieur but the *Provisional Government that had pieces of evidence in its hands.* Who lied, you or them? It claims to have the evidence, and so do you. It says it is publishing them for historical reasons; you declare you are using them as a means of *reprisal* against an enemy. Watch out! You seem to be eager for *reprisals.* Do you need them at whatever cost?

Imposture and ambush; these are the pivots of the intrigue cooked up against a man who disturbs you. Perfect, my good sirs; wretches used to purchasing with all crimes imaginable the favor of those in power forged a poisoned arm for your hatred. What that arm is worth, and whence it comes you know too well, and don't dare to touch it. But it goes along with the honor of your arrangements. Hidden in the wings. You toss the dagger into the hands of an assassin, laughing in advance at the useless blows your victim will waste on this mannequin.

Unfortunately, iniquity lied to itself. You should have ensured that your two Offices of Fraud were in agreement and not confound yourselves with your own work.

Fear perturbs perfidy's calculations. Your semi-official note sought to reduce me by this threat of reprisals, tempered with the insolent offer of recourse to your magnanimity. But you weren't reassured. One can't walk without care on the sinuous paths of calumny.

My response to intimidation was clear and swift, I think. Evidence in hand, before the public I showed that you had just turned over to Leopold the Belgian workers and refugees.

This proof of an act of coldly premeditated vengeance was greeted with cries of vengeance. This cry again threw terror into the Hotel de Ville; they already heard the rumblings of riot at their doors, and imposture in all its forms was called to the rescue. Rumors spread by a thousand mouths pointed to me as the author of a plot whose goal was the members of the Provisional Government. The news of my arrest circulated in all the clubs.

On the evening of March 30 Citizen X. Durrieu said to me, "Let's put our cards on the table. I come from the Provisional Government and here's what I learned: you want to overthrow it and assume a dictatorship. You will no doubt succeed, for the government has no strength, but you will then be destroyed, both you and France. Your project is folly. Renounce it and adopt that which I will propose to you and which brings together all your possibilities. The coterie of the *National* will be thrown out and you'll replace it with your friends. Come talk with Ledru-Rollin; this will be a simple thing, since you're former schoolmates."

To be sure such proposals surprised me in the presence of

the odious rumors spread around Paris. At least they proved to me that a part of the government rejected the slander cooked up by the reactionaries at bay.

An unheard of situation! On one side I am offered a hand to rise to power, and on the other they try to throw me into the abyss. Here the Capitol, there the Tarpeian Rock. Eight whole days this strange struggle took me from the heights to the depths. Finally it appeared that justice and truth won the day. An appointment was set with M. Ledru-Rollin for the 31st. But reaction was on the watch; it understood the imminence of danger. The very day of the 31st the fabricated evidence appeared in the *Revue Rétrospective*.

The gauntlet was thrown down. A fight to the death was engaged. Republicans, old soldiers of the old cause who have remained faithful to the flag of principle, you who haven't sold your consciences to the new masters in exchange for honors, money or positions, beware! Let my example be a warning to you. Today it is me, tomorrow it will be you. Woe on those who cause embarrassment. We will all be struck! In the head, the heart, in front, from behind it doesn't matter: we will be struck!

What is my crime? That of having confronted counter-revolution, of having unmasked its plans for six weeks, and of showing the people the danger around them that is growing, and that will engulf them all.

The wretches! They give orders to their *bravi* to drag me before the tribunals whose resignation I demanded yesterday. And who will be the accusers, the witnesses, the judges in this trial? Royalty's henchmen, become the henchmen of reaction. Those who tortured me twenty times will torment me again. Yesterday it was freedom, my life, today it's my honor; everything must be turned over to them so that they can devour their prey whole. With what pleasure they will tear apart what is left of their old, hated enemy. And all these agents of Louis-Philippe what is the reason they pretend to punish me? I, worn out, my hair turned white in the dungeons of Louis-Philippe! Who would believe this? To have treated with Louis-Philippe! And they set themselves up as avengers of the revolution!

The executioners of patriots, the golden mean's assassins are now the devotees, the faithful of the Hotel de Ville. The total due has been paid! There they are fulfilling the functions of the Forty-Five for the gentlemen of the Provisional Government, and they'll assassinate the republicans for the account of the republic, as they have done for so long for the account of the monarchy. Positions, happiness, fortune will soon be theirs. So much audacity six weeks after the barricades. Who could have guessed it?

Reactionaries of the Hotel de Ville, you are cowards! I stand in your way, and you want to kill me, but you don't dare attack me from the front, so you throw in my path three or four bassets from Louis-Philippe's pack who are in search of a new kennel. You egg them on from behind, far from the risk of splashes. Kindly accept my sincere compliments.

There are royalists among you. I forgive them. They are avenging the monarchy through one of its bitterest enemies. But there are also republicans, and to them I pose the question, their hands on their consciences: is it thus that they should be treating a veteran who buried half his life, his family, his affections in royalty's deepest dungeons?

If you had an accusation to make against me it should have been produced in broad daylight, solemnly, and surrounded with all guarantees of certainty, of authenticity. You should have spoken in the name of justice, of morality, without in any way declining the responsibility for such an act.

But you said it yourselves, these are reprisals you are carrying out. All methods are good in crushing a dangerous rival. Success at any price is your doctrine it seems, as it was for your predecessors. It appears that this document was necessary to you. *Is fecit cui prodest.* The infamy of its origins is betrayed by the shameful twists and turns of its publication. Reactionaries, you are cowards!

L-A Blanqui
La République, April 14,1848

For the Red Flag

We are no longer in '93! We are in 1848!

The tricolor flag is no longer the flag of the Republic. It's that of Louis-Philippe and of the monarchy.

It's the tricolor flag that presided over the massacres of the rue Transnonain, of faubourg de Vaise, of Saint-Etienne. It has been twenty times bathed in the blood of the workers.

The people raised the red colors on the barricades of '48, just as they raised them on those of June 1832, April 1834, and May 1839. They have received the double consecration of defeat and victory. From this day on, these colors are theirs.

Just yesterday they gloriously floated from the fronts of our buildings.

Today reaction ignominiously casts them in the mud and dares stain them with its calumnies.

It is said it is a flag of blood. It is only red with the blood of the martyrs who made it the standard of the republic.

Its fall is an insult to the people, a profanation of the dead. The flag of the National Guard will shade their graves.

Reaction has already been unleashed. It can be recognized by its violence. The men of the royalist faction roam the streets, insults and threats in their mouths, tearing the red colors from the boutonnieres of citizens.

Workers! It's your flag that is falling. Heed well! The Republic will not delay in following it.

To the Mountain of 1793! To the Pure Socialists, its True Heirs!

The Socialist Worker's Banquet took place Sunday December 3, 1848 at exactly noon at the Association of Cooks, 36 Barrière du Maine. 1,000 guests and 300-400 of the curious – 1,500 in all, among them 400-500 women, participated. The name of the Chairman of the banquet, Citizen A. Blanqui, held in the dungeon of Vincennes, could be read on the tribune across from the name of the candidate of the republican socialists, F-V Raspail. There could also be read on signs the names of those outlawed by reaction who are the most beloved of the people: Louis Blanc, Barbès, Albert.

Citizen Salières opened the session with these few words:

Citizens:

The Commission of the Socialist Worker's banquet has chosen as its Chairman Citizen Auguste Blanqui, held in the dungeon of Vincennes (applause).

This commission, composed of workers, calling workers to this fraternal banquet wants to testify in their name to its gratitude to this indefatigable combatant for democracy, this man who is the incessant victim of persecution because of his defense of the most noble of causes, whose pure devotion has been repaid with persecution and calumny.

Citizens, you know how overwhelmed socialism today is. The very people who, if socialism could be personified in one man, would attempt to cross that man from the book of life, these very people proclaim themselves to be socialists. They say they are its adherents and reject its true principles. This presents a great danger for us. The history of the ideas that in all eras have served to tie men together shows us that it is the same lovers of the form who have often stifled the idea, or at least have reduced it to petty proportions. And so we proletarians, we for whom the word "socialism" is synonymous with that of "liberation," have come here to present the true idea, the principle of socialism. We will do it in our way, with our hearts. We hope that you will take account of our efforts (Yes! Yes!)

After these words Citizen Salières read the prisoner's toast:

To the Mountain of 1793! To the Pure Socialists, its true heirs!

Citizens, the Mountain had sublime inspirations, daughters of the gospels and philosophy. But it never possessed those positive theories that only grow slowly from a close analysis of the social body, just as the art of healing is born of the revelations of anatomy.

Nevertheless, if it was lacking in the organizing force of science, the impulses of the heart sufficed to dictate to it the immortal slogan of the future: Liberty, Equality, Fraternity, and that admirable symbol, the Declaration of Rights, which broadly interpreted contains the seed of all that will come in the future society. Unfortunately, it's the fate of the works of genius that have shaken the world to perish asphyxiated under the clouds of incense under which superstitious admirers drown them. The vivifying spirit of the master dies suffocated by the narrow observance of the text. The Law of Moses succumbed to the desperate embrace of the Pharisees. The Koran will be extinguished, turned into stone by the immobility of its imbecilic sectarians. And the Gospels themselves would have been sealed in their tomb by the idolatrous hands of its disciples – who had become its gravediggers – if their immortal ideas, escaping from the icy corpse around which they knelt, had not reappeared ever more shining in the new incarnation that will perpetuate them among humanity.

The Declaration of Rights, a formula born yesterday, is already suffering the fate of the old dogmas which in their period of decrepitude almost always become instruments of reaction against the redemptory labors of their revealers. The Judaic cult of the letter killed the revolutionary spirit of the symbol.

The militant life of the Mountain was brief, and like that of Christ ended on Golgotha. But its acts are a sparkling commentary on its words and provide the true meaning of the teachings it spread around the world.

Like Jesus, the consoler of the poor, the enemy of the powerful, the Mountain loved those who suffer and hated those who caused suffering. The salient element of its existence was its intimate alliance with the Parisian proletariat, not because it only felt the pain of one city, but because among so many populations equally bent down by suffering it found this energetic group ready at hand for the fight, for it was moved by the consciousness of its sufferings, and it made of them the liberating army of the human race.

From August 10, the date of the fall of the monarchy, until 4 Prairial, the final convulsion of the faubourgs, the people and the Mountain marched as one across the revolution, inseparable in victory and defeat. What a marvelous role to assume again! And one all the easier because the fight of 1793 was taken up again in 1848, on the same battlefield between the same combatants and , strange as it might seem, with almost the same incidents.

What do we see? As in 1793 privilege in combat with equality, and as their champions in combat a reactionary legislative majority colliding with the masses of Parisian democracy.

Will we also again find the Mountain and its faithful brotherhood in arms with the people?

And in fact, the name has reappeared! All the soldiers of

the young phalanx bear it with pride and swear to bravely follow the steps of their predecessors.

Silence! The gates swing open and the action begins.

What do I hear! Under the pretext of fraternity M. Ledru-Rollin, the new leader of the Holy Mountain imperiously demands the return of the troops to the capitol against the will of the people. Is this in any way the tradition of the Mountain? I open my history book and I read that the Gironde, trembling in anger and fright before the pressure of the faubourgs, having demanded the formation of a camp of 20,000 men at the city gates to cover the national representatives, the Mountain rose up against this project fatal to freedom, set the multitude in motion, threatened the majority, and finally gained victory in this life or death question. Paris remained free.

We were less fortunate. And yet, turning the soldiers away from the bloody arena of civil war, where they could only harvest hatred and death, signified treating them as brothers. The men of the Mountain preferred fraternization in the streets.

What do we see now? The people marching in columns from the Champ de Mars to the Hotel de Ville and M. Ledru-Rollin, leader of the Mountain, has them run the gauntlet between two ranks of bayonets. And then he sets counter-revolution on the anarchists. I never saw this maneuver in either Marat's or Danton's campaigns. On that day did the hero of the recall of the troops incorrectly read his Montagnard theory?

And then there was another adventure. Who is that on horseback at the head of the National Guard? It's M. Ledru-Rollin, leader of the Mountain leading victorious reaction to the Hotel de Ville and the patriot prisoners to the dungeon of Versailles.

Is it possible? Is it also M. Ledru-Rollin who presents and the Mountain who vote the draconian law against public gatherings? It is!

Good god! Are these Montagnards nothing but Girondins? But I read the name of Robespierre on their hats.

Be patient. Faithful to the parallels, no scene of the past will be missing from today's drama. As in the past the mounting tide of hostilities between a reactionary majority and the Parisian workers must inevitably lead to a May 31. It broke out not on May 15, a grotesque day, but on June 23.

The army of the Mountain was ready on that day. And what did we see? Our monkeys of the Mountain throwing away their liberty bonnets and other revolutionary garb, inciting from the four corners all the stored up anger of the federalists, and like an avalanche, precipitating the counter-revolutionary masses on Paris.

The affront of May 31 was avenged; the rebellious Babylon punished. And by whom? By the Mountain!

Woe on the defeated. Those of June drank the chalice to the dregs. Crimes are eagerly being imputed to them. Had they emerged victorious everyone would have asked for a place of honor behind their flag. They are dead, and everyone spits anathema on them. Reaction says they are escapees from penal colonies and the Mountain says they are in the pay of monarchism.

What was the point of this last outrage? What is the goal of the fable of Russian gold and the ridiculous voyage in search of dynastic employment? As if royalty could today move a single paving stone. Why this pathetic tactic which makes friends and enemies laugh with pity? Most likely to prevent any solidarity with the defeated. But everyone knows there is nothing in common between you and them. Your artillery has sufficiently proved your innocence. Perhaps your artillery has to be justified in the eyes of some others, and so you go seeking imaginary leaders at the expense of the honor of the dead.

You dare to say that the Parisian people, the precursors of

the future, are nothing but a herd of animals that Pitt and Cobourg lead to the slaughterhouse with a handful of salt. And all this because it pleased M. Ledru-Rolin to harangue them in the form of cannon fire. Fire, gentlemen, but don't slander. June 26 is one of those ill-fated days that the revolution takes credit for in tears, just as a mother calls for the corpse of her son.

All of you, you great unknowns, who are swallowed up by the mass graves, poor Lazaruses fallen before the bullets in the great hunt for those in rags, you were nothing but the tools and mercenaries of royalism! You too, monuments to the justice and the clemency of our masters, unfortunate victims of prison ships. Colfavru, Thuillier, writers struck from behind, noble martyrs of the press for whom the press had not one word of protection or farewell. And you my old companions of Mont Saint Michel: Jarasse, Herbulet, Pétremann, valiant soldiers of May and February, thrice guilty of the crime of lack of respect for the army, know there in your lion's pit that the kabyle razzia swept you up as enemies of the republic.

And the saviors of the republic, the Brutuses and Scaevolas are the generals and aides-de-camp of Louis-Philippe, the marquis of the Faubourg Saint-Germain, the holy militias of the congregations. But also the glorious decorated of June, all of them furious newly-minted royalists, the princes and dukes, intrepid leaders of the rural National Guard. And finally, there's the Chouans who rose up en masse at the call of their priests to attack Paris. Did they do this to avenge '93, to avenge the old insults of the impious city? Not at all! It was to defend the republic against the Parisian royalist brigands!

O old formulas! Will of the wisps that cause the mountains to sink into the marshes. This is the result of your blows! You've turned our senators into vicars and marabouts murmuring prayers they no longer understand. But this isn't your fault. You have always been clear about things, but the Mountain's senses have been weakened.

The world has moved on in fifty years, but they have remained immobile. Science has forged more certain weapons, cleared a wider and more direct road. But the Mountain persists in walking down the paths of the past in old worn out attire, and they cry out against any novelty unknown to our fathers. These Epimenides fell asleep during a session of the Convention and upon awakening inadvertently took their place on the benches of the right. And then there they come, playing the year 1793 before the public, with its words, costumes and decors, everything except the play's meaning, like those Ellevious and Malibran of Quimper-Corentin who think they'll find the voices they need in the costume room.

The first act opened with the decree of vests à la Robespierre. The show goes on, and we will be spared not a couplet or a line. The least change in the script will result in its criminal author being sent before the revolutionary tribunal.

Our Epimenides recognize no other living beings than the dead of 1793, and whether they want it or not they assign everyone a role in their play. At the current moment it's the second Cordelier Club that's on stage. A deputy (infinitely newer in the Taitbout Room than today on Rue Taitbout) having gotten sensed the presence of the first version and denounced a Hébertist conspiracy, the men of the Mountain immediately set out on their trail.

They swear that in order to fool the bloodhounds who are after them the guilty have changed their names; that Hébert is now called Proudhon and Chaumette Raspail. They are searching everywhere for disguised versions of Ronsin, Momoro, Vincent, Anacharsis Cloots, Bishop Gobel. Watch out for the priest of Saint Eustache, who is a socialist. I advise him if he falls into their hands that if he wants to come out of this safe to protest that he is not Father Gobel, but rather the abbot Gregoire, and then he'll be smothered in excuses and caresses.

The Jacobins asked M. Buchez to illuminate their

97

searches with his parliamentary history lantern. Imagine their surprise when he angrily answered them: "There's no need to seek; it is you who are the Hébertists since you don't admire the Saint Bartholomew's massacre."

It appears that at the moment of the abrupt awakening of February 24 all of the sleepers carried out a confused exchange of heads, to such an extent that in the midst of this chaos of unmatched physiognomies the disoriented M. Buchez takes Girondins for Hébertists, the former thinking themselves to be men of the Mountain.

People then ran to seek information from Pierre Leroux, the author of the "Renaissance dans l'Humanité." But the good patriarch gently told his questioners that without any doubt individuals are indefinitely reborn from generation to generation, but perfected and better; that consequently there were no more, there could no longer be, either Girondins, men of the Mountain, or Hébertists.

The response convinced no one and the searches are actively continuing. We already have proof that "Le Peuple" the newspaper of Hébert-Proudhon is nothing but the former "Père Duchêne" disguising its style.

These buffooneries would be funny if they hadn't become tragic. Unfortunately, in this play every scene of uncontrollable laughter immediately engenders a scene of tears and blood. The actors themselves don't know the denouement of their performance. In all good faith they thought they were presenting it for the profit and not at the expense of the workers. They will perhaps console themselves for the misadventure with the thought that they were performing in a play with two ends, one happy and the other sad, and that all that is wrong flows from an error in the variant.

But this mass of unexpected incidents, of situations improvised outside and against the libretto, seriously demoralizes them and leads them to dream about the fickleness of the public.

Political romanticism has most decidedly perverted people's spirits. In no condition to resist the torrent and maintain the classical tradition in its integrity, the academicians of the Mountain painfully resign themselves to make a sacrifice to the folly of the day and dress the old repertoire in the taste of today.

Rags cut from Proudhon, Leroux, Cabet and Fourier have been sewed onto Robespierre's worn out coat, and from this variety they've put together the most eclectic of picturesque and vulgar costumes, a harlequin's costume, now hung as a sign at the doors of the theater and carried in great pomp around the streets for the edification of the crowd.

On the breast of the mannequin, spread in trompe l'oeil, shine the socialist labels, to the great chagrin of their legitimate owners, the innovators who see their formulas turned into advertisements for the Hotel des Invalides.

These fraudulent borrowings force us to lengthen our motto with endless epithets. Is it not disastrous to call oneself by a name more interminable than that of a Spanish grandee and to need a half an hour to issue one's rallying cry?

We are victims of the most abominable of ambushes. It is we socialists, the so-called despoilers, who everyone despoils at will and with no shame. Even our name has been taken from us, and soon our shadows will be stolen. What is more, the men of the Mountain, reaction's youngest children, in pillaging us have done nothing but follow the example of their elders. If today they steal our title of socialist, yesterday the others wrested our title of republican.

Yes, this noble name of republican, outlawed and ridiculed by the counter revolution, was imprudently stolen by them so they could crown themselves with the laurel of our victory. With the same audacity they stole from us our sublime slogan of Liberty, Equality, Fraternity, so long insulted and covered with mud by them as the symbol of blood and death.

Fortunately it rejected our flag... This was a mistake: It remains ours.

Citizens, the Mountain is dead!

To socialism, its sole heir!

Warning to the People

What reef menaces tomorrow's revolution?

The reef that broke that of yesterday: the deplorable popularity of bourgeois disguised as tribunes of the people.

Ledru-Rollin, Louis Blanc, Crémieux, Lamartine, Garnier-Pagé, Dupont de l'Eure, Flocon, Albert, Arago, Marrast!

A dismal list! Sinister names written in blood on the paving stones of democratic Europe.

The provisional government killed the Revolution. It is upon its head that the responsibility for all these disasters, for the blood of so many thousands of victims must fall.

Reaction is doing nothing but its job in cutting democracy's throat.

The crime is that of the traitors the trusting people accepted as guides, but who instead gave them reaction.

Miserable government! Despite screams and prayers, it decrees the 45 centime tax that causes the desperate countryside to rise up; it keeps in place the royalist headquarters, the royalist magistrates, the royalist laws. Treason!

It runs down the workers of Paris; April 15 it imprisons those of Limoges; it guns down those of Rouen on the 27th; it sets loose all its executioners; it deceives and tracks down all sincere republicans. Treason! Treason!

To it alone belongs the terrible burden of all of the calamities that have all but wiped out the Revolution

Oh, these are the real guilty ones, the guiltiest among the guilty; those the deceived people saw as its sword and shield; those it acclaimed with enthusiasm, the judges of its future.

What a misfortune it would be for us if, on the

forthcoming day of the people's victory, the forgetful indulgence of the masses allows a single one of these men who forfeited their mandate to take power! That, for a second time, would be the end of the revolution.

Let the workers always have before their eyes this list of accursed names! And if even one should ever appear in a government that is a product of the insurrection, let them all cry out with one voice: treason!

Speeches, sermons, and programs would only be frauds and lies; the same jugglers will return to perform the same act, with the same bag of tricks; they would form the first link of a new, more furious chain of reaction!

Anathema on them, should they ever dare reappear!

Shame and pity on the imbecilic mass which would again fall into their net!

It's not enough that the thieves of February be ejected for good from the Hotel de Ville; we must be protected against new traitors.

That government would be treasonous which, raised upon the proletarian bulwark, doesn't instantly carry out:

1. The disarmament of the bourgeois guards,

2. The armament and organization of a national militia of all workers.

There are doubtless other indispensable measures, but they will grow naturally from this first act, which is the preliminary guarantee, the only pledge of security for the people.

There must remain not one rifle in the hands of the bourgeoisie. Without this, there is no salvation.

The diverse doctrines which today dispute among themselves for the sympathy of the masses can one day fulfil their promises of betterment and well being, on condition they not abandon the prey for its shadow.

Arms and organization, these are the decisive elements of progress, *the* serious method for putting an end to misery.

Who has iron, has bread.

We prostrate ourselves before the bayonets; they sweep up the disarmed crowd. France bristling with workers in arms means the advent of socialism.

In the presence of armed workers obstacles, resistances, and impossibilities will all disappear.

But for those workers who allow themselves to be amused by ridiculous strolls in the street, by the planting of liberty trees, by the mellifluous phrases of lawyers, there will first be holy water, then insults, and, finally, the gun. And misery forever.

Let the people choose!

Proclamation of February 20, 1866

Given the declaration by the Minister of War, dated [blank] December 1851, signed Leroy and Saint-Arnaud, which states:

"All individuals taken arms in hand will be executed."

Given that following the criminal attack of December 2, 1851 those prisoners who were defenders of the constitution were put to death during and after the combat;

That in diverse places in the capitol a crowd of citizens, inoffensive and without arms; innocent bystanders, were killed at the hands of the Praetorian guards;

That on the boulevard, a mass of peaceful spectators, men, women and children were suddenly and without provocation massacred by Bonaparte's soldiery;

That this same soldiery slaughtered, in their homes, without distinction of either age or sex, the residents of several houses;

That in the departments of the Herault, Ain and the Nievre, the defenders of the constitution were, not gunned down, but guillotined by sentence of the Councils of War, well after the end of the struggle;

Given that in the presence of these crimes the magnanimity which the people has shown over the last forty years during civil wars would from here on in be both a crime and an act of suicide.

The commander-in-chief of the Republican army declares:

Article 1 – Bonaparte, his ministers, the legislature and the senate are declared public enemies;

Article 2 – All government functionaries are suspended from their duties. All violators will be executed;

Article 3 – All police officers and agents are to remain at home. Those who appear on the streets, in uniform or otherwise, will be executed;

Article 4 – Those officers who are members of a body that fired on the people will be executed;

Article 5 – Officers, non-commissioned officers and soldiers of any artillery regiment that fired on houses so as to set them on fire, will be executed;

Article 6 – Those non-commissioned officers and soldiers who fired on the people will be sent to the colonies. Those who massacred children, women, or the elderly will be executed;

Article 7 – All soldiers are called upon to shoot down any chief who orders that the people be fired upon;

Article 8 – Those officers who, during the struggle, declare themselves for the republic, will receive a large reward as a sign of national gratitude;

Article 9 – Those soldiers and non-commissioned officers who, during the struggle, embrace the Republican cause will have a right either to leave the army, or to promotion to a higher rank within the national army. Upon leaving each soldier will receive 300 francs beyond his departure bonus, each non-commissioned officer 500 francs.

Proclamation to Parisians

Parisians:

Sixteen years of gags! Sixteen years of outrages! France scoffed at, pillaged, trampled upon! Wasn't that enough? No! Now hunger tears at the guts of the people!

Bonaparte promised glory and prosperity. Prosperity! Yes, he alone devoured 400 million francs, 25 million a year, 70,000 francs a day. He gorged with gold his Mamelukes, speculators, camp followers, priests. All he left to you to satisfy your hunger, was the rubble of demolitions.

Glory! We know it: Mexico, Mentana. And that's only a beginning. From here on out all soldiers between 20 and 30 are soldiers...soldiers of the Pope.

They'll have the honor of dying for the Jesuits, and Father Hyacinthe promises to hear their confessions on the battlefield.

To those who escape that glory, they'll distribute soup at the doors of churches and barracks.

No more workshops! No more marriages! All of that is revolutionary. Nothing but palaces and prisons, convents and whorehouses!....

To arms, Parisians! Enough is enough! You received freedom from your fathers; you will not leave servitude to your sons.

The oppressors have filled the cup to the brim. To arms! Let punishment fall like lightning on their outrages. The hour of the great revolution of the people has sounded! Let us march!

Manual for an Armed Insurrection

This program is purely military and leaves entirely to the side the political and social question, which this isn't the place for: besides, it goes without saying, that the revolution must (effectively work against the tyranny of the capital, and) reconstitute society on the basis of justice.

A Parisian insurrection which repeats the old mistakes no longer has any chance of success today.

In 1830, popular fervor alone was enough to bring down a power surprised and terrified by an armed insurrection, an extraordinary event, which had one chance in a thousand.

That was good once. The lesson was learnt by the government, which remained monarchical and counter-revolutionary, although it was the result of a revolution. They began to study street warfare, and the natural superiority of art and discipline over inexperience and confusion was soon re-established.

However, it will be said, in 1848 the people triumphed using the methods of 1830. So be it. But let us not have any illusions! The victory of February [1830] was nothing but a stroke of luck. If Louis-Philippe had seriously defended himself, supremacy would have remained with the uniforms.

The proof is the June days. It is here that one can see how disastrous were the tactics, or rather the absence of tactics of the insurrection. Never had they had such a favourable position: ten chances against one.

On one side, the Government in total anarchy, demoralized troops: on the other, all the workers were solid and almost certain of success. Why did they succumb? Owing to lack of organisation. To account for their defeat, it is enough to analyze their strategy.

The uprising breaks out. At once, in the workers' districts, the barricades go up here and there, aimlessly, at a multitude of points.

Five, ten, twenty, thirty, fifty men, brought together by chance, the majority without weapons, they start to overturn carriages, dig up paving stones and pile them up to block the roads, sometimes in the middle of a street, more often at intersections. Many of these barriers would present hardly any obstacle to the cavalry.

Sometimes, after the crude beginnings of preparing their defenses, the builders leave to go in the search of rifles and ammunition.

In June, one could count more than sixty barricades; about thirty or so alone carried the burdens of the battle. Of the others, nineteen or twenty did not fire a shot. From there, glorious bulletins made a lot of noise about the removal of fifty barricades, where there was not a soul.

While some are tearing the paving stones from the streets, other small bands are disarming the *corps de garde* or seizing gunpowder and weapons from the armories. All this is done without coordination or direction, at the mercy of individual imagination.

Little by little, however, a certain number of barricades, higher, stronger, better built, are chosen by defenders, who concentrate there. It is not calculation, but chance which determines the site of these principal fortifications. Just a few, by a kind of military inspiration rather than design, occupy the large intersections.

During this first period of the insurrection, the troops, on their side, gather. The generals receive and study the police reports. They take good care not to let their detachments venture out without unquestionable data, for fear of failure which would demoralize the soldiers. As soon as they have determined the

110

positions of the insurrectionists, they mass the regiments at various points which will constitute from now on the base of their operations.

Both armies are in position. Let us look at their manoeuvres. Here will be laid bare the vice of popular tactics, the undoubted cause of the disaster.

Neither direction nor general command, not even coordination between the combatants. Each barricade has its particular group, more or less numerous, but always isolated. Whether it numbers ten or one hundred men, it does not maintain any communication with the other positions. Often there is not even a leader to direct the defence, and if there is, his influence is next to nil. The fighters do whatever comes into their head. They stay, they leave, they return, according to their good pleasure. In the evening, they go to sleep.

In consequence of these continual comings and goings, the number of citizens remaining at the barricades varies rapidly by a third, a half, sometimes by three quarters. Nobody can count on anybody. From this grows distrust of their capacity to succeed and thus, discouragement.

Nothing is known of what is happening elsewhere and they do not trouble themselves further. Rumors circulate, some black, some rosy. They listen peaceably to the cannons and the gunfire, while drinking at the wine merchants. As for sending relief to the positions under attack, there is not even the thought of it. "Let each defends his post, and all will be well," say the strongest. This singular reasoning is because the majority of the insurgents fight in their own district, a capital fault which has disastrous consequences, in particular the denunciation by their neighbors, after the defeat.

For with such a system, defeat is certain. It comes at the end in the person of two or three regiments which fall upon the barricade and crush their few remaining defenders. The whole battle is just the monotonous repetition of this invariable maneuver. While the insurrectionists smoke their pipes behind heaps of paving stones, the enemy successively concentrates all his forces against one point, then on to a second, a third, a fourth, and thereby exterminates the insurrection one bit at a time.

The popular fighters do not take care to counter this easy task. Each group awaits its turn philosophically and would not venture to run to the aid of a neighbor in danger. No! "He will defend his post; he cannot give up his post."

This is how one perishes through absurdity!

When, thanks to such grave faults, the great Parisian revolt of 1848 was shattered like glass by the most pitiful of governments, what catastrophe should we not fear if we begin again with the same stupidity, before a savage militarism, which now has in its service the recent conquests of science and technology: railways, the electric telegraph, rifled cannon, the breech-loading rifles?

For example, something we should not count as one of the new advantages of the enemy is the strategic thoroughfares which now furrow the city in all the directions. They are feared, but wrongly. There is nothing about them to be worried about. Far from having created a danger for the insurrection, as people think, on the contrary they offer a mixture of disadvantages and advantages for the two parties. If the troops circulate with more ease along them, on the other hand they are also heavily exposed and in the open.

Such streets are unusable under gunfire. Moreover, balconies are miniature bastions, providing lines of fire on their flanks, which ordinary windows do not. Lastly, these long straight avenues deserve perfectly the name of boulevard that is given to them. They are indeed true boulevards, which constitute the natural front of a very great strength.

The weapon par excellence in street warfare is the rifle. The cannon makes more noise than effect. Artillery could have serious impact only by the use of incendiaries. But such an atrocity, employed systematically on a large scale, would soon turn against its authors and would be to their loss.

The grenade, which people have the bad habit of calling a bomb, is generally secondary, and subject besides to a mass of disadvantages. It consumes a lot of powder for little effect, is very dangerous to handle, has no range and can only be used from windows. Paving stones do almost as much harm but are not so expensive. The workers do not have money to waste.

For the interior of houses, the revolver and the bayonet, sword, sabre and dagger. In a boarding house, a pike or eight-foot long halberd would triumph over the bayonet.

The army has only two great advantages over the people: the breech-loading rifle and organisation. This last especially is immense, irresistible. Fortunately one can deprive him of this advantage, and in this case ascendancy passes to the side of the insurrection.

In civil disorders, with rare exceptions soldiers march only with loathing, by force and brandy. They would like to be elsewhere and more often look behind than ahead. But an iron hand retains them as slaves and victims of a pitiless discipline; without any affection for authority, they obey only fear and are lacking in any initiative. A detachment which is cut off is a lost detachment. The commanders are not unaware of this, and worry above all to maintain communication between all their forces. This need cancels out a portion of their manpower.

In the popular ranks, there is nothing like this. There one fights for an idea. There only volunteers are found, and what drives them is enthusiasm, not fear. Superior to the adversary in devotion, they are much more still in intelligence. They have the upper hand over him morally and even physically, by conviction, strength, fertility of resources, promptness of body and spirit, they have both the head and the heart. No troop in the world is the equal of these elite men.

So what do they lack in order to vanquish? They lack the unity and coherence which, by having them all contribute to the same goal, fosters all those qualities which isolation renders impotent. They lack organisation. Without it, they haven't got a chance. Organisation is victory; dispersion is death.

June 1848 put this truth beyond question. What would be the case today? With the old methods, the entire people would succumb should the troops decide to hold out, and they will hold out, so long as they see before them only irregular forces, without direction. On the other hand, the very sight of a Parisian army in good order operating according to tactical regulations would strike the soldiers dumb and make them drop their resistance.

A military organisation, especially when it has to be improvised on the battle field, is no small business for our party. It presupposes a commander-in-chief and, up to a certain point, the usual series of officers of all ranks. Where to find this personnel? Revolutionary and socialist middle-class men are rare and the few that there are fight only the war of the pen. These gentlemen imagine they can turn the world upside down with their books and their newspapers, and for sixteen years they have scribbled as far as the eye can see, without being tired out by their difficulties; with an equine patience, they suffer the bit, the saddle and the riding crop, and never a kick! Damn that! Return the blows? That's for louts.

These heroes of the inkstand profess the same scorn for the sword as officers for their slices of bread and butter. They do not seem to suspect that force is the only guarantee of freedom; that people are slaves wherever the citizens are ignorant of art of soldiery and give up the privilege to a caste or a corporate body.

In the republics of antiquity, among the Greeks and Romans, everyone knew and practiced the art of war. The professional soldier was an unknown species. Cicero was a general, Caesar a lawyer. By taking off the toga and donning the uniform, they would begin as colonel or captain and would acquit themselves ably. As long as it is not the same in France, we will remain civilians fit to be cut down at mercy of the officer caste.

Thousands of the educated young, working-class and bourgeois tremble under a detested yoke. To break it, do they think of taking up the sword? No! The pen, always the pen, only the pen. Why the one and not the other, as the duty of a republican requires? In times of tyranny, to write is fine, to fight is better, when the enslaved pen remains powerless. *Eh bien*, no! They publish a pamphlet, then go into prison, but they do not think of opening a manual of military tactics, to learn there in twenty-four hours the trade which constitutes all the power of our oppressors, and which would put in our hands our revenge and their punishment.

But what is the good of these complaints? it is the stupid practice of our time to deplore something instead of doing something about it. Jeremiads are the fashion. Jeremiah poses in all the attitudes, he cries, whips, he dogmatizes, he dominates, he thunders, the plague of all plagues. Let us leave these elegizers, these grave-diggers of freedom! The duty of a revolutionist is the fight, the fight come what may, the fight until death.

Do the cadres lack for the forming of an army? *Eh bien!* We must improvise them on the ground even, in the course of action. The people of Paris will provide all the elements, former soldiers, ex-national guards. Their scarcity will oblige us to reduce to a minimum the number of officers and NCOs. But no matter. The zeal, the ardor, the intelligence of the volunteers, will make up for this deficit.

The essential thing is to organize. No more of these tumultuous risings, with ten thousand isolated heads, acting at random, in disorder, without any overall design, each in their local area and acting according to their own whim! No more of these ill-conceived and badly made barricades, which waste time, encumber the streets, and block circulation, as necessary to one party as the other. As much as the troops, the Republican must have freedom of his movements.

No useless racing about, hurly-burly, clamoring! Every minute and every step is equally precious. Above all, do not hole up in our own district as the insurrectionists have never failed to do, to their great harm. This mania, after having caused the defeat, facilitates proscriptions. We must cure ourselves of this under penalty of catastrophe.

The Army Enslaved and Oppressed

Following the hideous discoveries that are currently provoking public indignation, the guilty — supported by the usual traitors — have impudently taken the offensive and cry out with all their might: "All for the insulted army!" Which should be translated as: "All against the lack of respect for the big brass."

The army! For the last eight years these same traitors have constantly nailed it to the pillory. For the last eight years all Frenchmen have been voters, except prisoners and soldiers. This is the real insult to the army!

The republic granted suffrage to those with no criminal record. Could it refuse it to the brave men who give the fatherland their blood and their freedom? As a reward for such a sacrifice, can it cross them off the list of citizens? The republic didn't have the beautiful idea of assimilating men under to the flag to evildoers. Soldiers can vote.

But here's the thing. Since the "bloody week," when the men at headquarters (who are Jesuits) had the Parisians massacred by the Chouans, most of the non-commissioned officers and soldiers have given their votes to republican candidates. Every new election was a patriotic conquest. In certain garrisons the difference in the number of votes between the two military parties was as much as ten or eleven to one. If civilian voters had done the same, in just a little while the republic would have carried off the victory. The officers were furious, and the reactionaries concerned. This meant a farewell to their hopes to erect the throne with the help of the army. This meant a farewell to the perpetual refrain of conservatives: "the only resource left to us are the troops."

This beautiful dream was going to fade away thanks to the votes in the cartridge bags of soldiers that turned against them. But those worthies preferred bullets to this fate. And in a gesture of high treason the so-called National Assembly improvised this evil metamorphosis. The free thinker prostrated himself before slavish thought.

This so-called National Assembly will answer to future legislatures of France. It will answer for having its power usurped in order to take — with the most perverse intentions- universal suffrage from the army, though they saw it as entirely favorable to the cause of progress and liberty.

Yes, to be sure it will have to render some serious accounts, at least if the executive and the legislative don't enter into a coalition to cap off all the lies, violence, and evil doings that have unfurled over the last ten years with a final coup d'état.

Without a doubt in this case the nation will find a way, for the crime is obvious. It dates from the month of July 1872 and was accomplished with a mixture of hypocrisy and shamelessness that is beyond all measure.

The French will remember that as soldiers and citizens they have constantly shown loyalty, patience, moderation, in painful contrast with the perfidy and the ferocity of their rulers.

The following report on the creation of a sitting national army will prove what should be and what will be the surest safeguard against external aggression and internal Machiavellianism.